I Wish I Worked There!

A LOOK INSIDE THE MOST CREATIVE SPACES IN BUSINESS

KURSTY GROVES WITH WILL KNIGHT | PHOTOGRAPHY BY EDWARD DENISON

This edition first published 2010
© 2010 John Wiley & Sons Ltd

Registered office
John Wiley & Sons Ltd, The Atrium, Southern Gate, Chichester,
West Sussex, PO19 8SQ, United Kingdom

For details of our global editorial offices, for customer services
and for information about how to apply for permission to reuse
the copyright material in this book please see our website at
www.wiley.com.

Executive Commissioning Editor: Helen Castle
Project Editor: Miriam Swift
Assistant Editor: Calver Lezama

ISBN 978-0-470-71383-9

Cover design, page design and layouts by Jeremy Tilston,
The Oak Studio Ltd
Printed in Italy by Printer Trento Srl

DEDICATION

In loving memory of Uncle Derrick

ACKNOWLEDGEMENTS

Thank you to the 38 companies that opened their doors and welcomed us in. To the 311 people interviewed, and to those who kindly arranged tours, lunches, coffees, cheeky rides on golf carts, extra chocolate chip cookies, and of course those who worked hard to help us to gain clearances and permissions.

Thanks also to our editor, Helen Castle, whose patience, kind support and grammar guidance made this mammoth task achievable. And to Ed Denison, for inspiring us to take on this crazy thing, but more importantly for being there from start to finish: 47,550 miles, over 10,000 photographs, and 2 babies later.

Big thanks goes to the 'connectors', without whom we'd not have any companies to visit: Lisa Buckley, Karen Callaghan, Rich Cawthray, Chris Dyball, Jules Gruzelier, Joseph Ingram, Stef Ingram, Joanna Ivison, Hamish Kinniburgh, Ryan Lynch, Gareth Miles, Ian O'Sullivan, Jon Peachey, Julie Peters, Ivy Ross, Steve Seabolt, Adrian Simpson, Bruce Vaughn, Fredrick Weiss and Dave Wykes.

To the people who have given us a creative space to write in along the way: Trish & John, Carolyn & Phil, Bill & Carolyn, Kristina & Bret. To the people who fed us, put us up (and put up with us): Alice & Ben, Tweed & Ash, Rich & Tash, Jock & Anne, Ed & Guang-Yu, Rick & Sab, The Watts family, Steve & Meredith, Greg & Vicky, Fiona & Steve, Nik & Kirsty, Lawrence & Emma, Dave & Karen, Dan & Liz, Big Dog.

To those who read, fed-back and encouraged us throughout: Hanne Kristiansen, Rachel Botsman, Trish, John, Ellie, Carolyn (mum), Bill, Carolyn, Phil Shade, Julian Swan, Emma-May Morely, Sejal Parekh, Matt Jackson. And to our friends at ?What If!, old and new, especially Chris Barez-Brown, Simon Bray, Nina Powell, Andy Reid and Sarah Dryden and the rest of those bright, passionate people who taught us a lot about innovation, energy and the importance of having fun.

Thank you also to the team who helped to pull the book together, shape it, polish it and get it out there: Miriam Swift, Lorna Mein, Calver Lezama, Alicia Barker, Emma Knott, Iain Campbell, Oliver Arnott, Jeremy Tilston and Midas PR.

Thank you Guang-Yu and Ella for the loan of Ed/baba. And thank you Jack: you were the 'bump' in this journey, yet you made the whole thing so much fun!

Thank you all so very much; it has been an epic journey and one from which we're still buzzing.

CONTENTS

CASE STUDIES

FOREWORD
IVY ROSS

Everyone wants to occupy creative space; yet few people are aware of the importance that 'place' plays in the nurturing of the creative process. My experience has proven that an environment which encourages a team to build trust and to play freely is an essential ingredient for innovation.

I have run product design and brand development departments in diverse companies over the last 30 years, including Coach, Mattel, Calvin Klein, Old Navy and Gap. My work became known in innovation circles. I appeared on the cover of *Fast Company magazine* for founding, in the late 1990s, a think tank named Project Platypus at Mattel Toys. The environment for Project Platypus differed greatly from that of the rest of the company. In this unique place, a short walk across the street from Mattel's headquarters, I supported groups of 12 employees for 12 weeks. Each group generated excitingly innovative concepts that created many opportunities for Mattel. For this work, I received the Chairman's Award for Sustainability.

Project Platypus became the inspiration for the clay street project, Procter & Gamble's off-site ideas incubator. The clay street project is one of the many case studies in *I Wish I Worked There!*. By presenting case studies from a wide range of successful companies, this book encourages the reader to experience the connection between the design of physical space and its impact on culture as well as on innovation that can be generated and sustained over time. It also reinforces the fact that creative spaces are cost effective by showing that budget boundaries can motivate some of the most unique solutions for leveraging entrepreneurial spirit.

Through its writing and photographs, *I Wish I Worked There!* explores various themes common to the unique creative environments of different companies. Examples include communal areas, such as kitchens and living room-like places that serve as informal gathering spaces. These areas encourage open and unbiased interaction between co-workers. Moreover, if the spaces have flexible floor plans and adaptable furniture, they encourage imaginative thinking and, in the rearranging, a renewal of 'innocence'. A desk shuffle every six months gives employees a chance to sit next to a different person. As the author observes in the book, it provides 'a re-boot' of people's workspaces to bring fresh eyes to a problem. Thus, the spaces themselves offer an unrestricted environment that people can modify to enhance innovation as concepts grow and change.

The author explores the inclusion of objects within the workspace that, in appealing to our sensory aesthetics, inspire a variety of passions among the people who work there. Another recurring theme is that of nature brought indoors, whether through bathing a room in natural light, setting up picnic benches or simply installing a green 'grass' carpet. This simple yet elegant approach helps to create a sense of endless possibilities.

These are just a few examples of the themes the author thoughtfully identifies and describes. This book becomes its own creative space by offering a series of diverse individual stories that you will find not only inspiring but filled with surprises.

INTRODUCTION
KURSTY GROVES

'The company that builds a culture of innovation is on the path to growth; the company that fails to innovate is on the path to obsolescence.'
AG Lafley and Ram Charan, from *The Game-Changer*

Why is it that some businesses seem to thrive by successfully nurturing a climate of innovation while others lose their competitive edge because they overlook the importance of creativity in their corporate environment? This question has long intrigued me and my colleagues over the years, leading me to form Headspace Consulting which specialises in creative spaces for business. As a designer and innovation consultant working with a wide variety of companies across industry – from beverages to investment banking, consumer goods to pharmaceuticals – I have spent time unlocking creative potential in people, only to see enthusiasm deflate as the reality of an environment filled with grey cubicles and corporate standards imposes its stultifying effect.

I am a believer in creative process and am fascinated by the idea that environment, both physical and cultural, can make or break creativity. I feel that it is possible to define what helps to cultivate creativity in a corporate environment: that the physical space can be used as a tool within the creative process, and is not a mystifying intangible that we can only hope to stumble upon. To test my assumptions I set myself the challenge of visiting some of the world's most successful brands and creative companies to better understand, at first hand, the various facets of physical environments that foster creativity, encourage ideas or knowledge sharing and allow fearless exploration.

After a year-long exhilarating global journey, engaging with many brilliant and impassioned minds and witnessing some genuinely inspirational workplaces, I was not simply taken aback by the extent to which my assumptions were confirmed, but I was dumbfounded by the sheer boundlessness of innovation employed by different people in different cultures with different limitations, united in the pursuit of innovation.

This book, as a record of that journey, takes a rare and privileged view behind the scenes of a deliberately wide range of companies, revealing how creativity is fostered by the built and cultural environment. It is as much a celebration of the creative process within these spaces as it is a manual for those seeking to improve their own workplace, whether in the spare room or in a multistorey office block.

At a time when innovation is a buzzword used all too liberally, and when the mantra 'innovate or die' rings uncomfortably in corporate executives' ears, economic realities are constantly weighing on the mind. Rather than regard innovation as an economic luxury, this book not only takes the stand that innovation and creativity should be among the primary corporate assets and the bedrock of any successful business, it also sets out to prove this unequivocally through extensive illustration of carefully selected case studies. For the first time ever, this book provides insights into the operations of some of the world's leading companies for whom the physical environment is understood to be a critical factor when it comes to the longevity and success of their business. After all, the environment is a company's second largest capital expense, next to its people, and arguably the second most powerful contributor to fostering creativity.

Throughout this journey, I visited companies I knew to be innovative and successful in their fields and that I had heard place an emphasis on the role of the environment in cultivating a happy and productive workplace for their people. What I did not know was how these environments would look. Would they be sexy, glamorous, super-chic, rough and ready or ultra-minimalist? All I knew was that creativity happens in these places. Some of the questions I was seeking to answer when visiting the companies included: How does the environment encourage day-to-day creativity? How do businesses support innovation initiatives? What do employees require in order to create? In revealing valuable insights, experiences and stories, this book shows that there is no one-size-fits-all solution, but there are recurring themes and principles that we can learn from. And of course, as with any great journey, there are plenty of surprises!

CREATIVE SPACES FOR CREATIVE ACTIVITY

As a result of this study I found that there are four main categories of creative space, each supporting a different type of creative activity. Every creative process we witnessed includes at least one of the following four creative activities: *stimulation*, where the mind is inspired or a thought process triggered in some new way; *reflection*, a period of uninterrupted focus; *collaboration*, where ideas are shared and built; and *play*, where experimentation occurs. Spaces that support these core creative activities come in all shapes and sizes; the following summary is intended to illustrate just a few examples.

SPACES THAT STIMULATE

Stimulating spaces expose the mind to a variety of stimuli – planned or random – in order to encourage people to think differently. The environment can be used as a tool to communicate an attitude: Virgin's vibrant graphics and bold statements express the creativity of the brand, bolstering a strong sense of identity. Stimulating environments can inspire a sense of awe through scale, as at Urban Outfitters' Navy Yard headquarters and Oakley's design bunker. They can immerse people in the subject for which they are creating, providing a more holistic view of the user. Nike's category co-location and Dyson's user course are great examples of this. Stimulating spaces such as those inhabited by Walt Disney's 'imagineers' can tell stories, drawing people deep into a curious, creative state. Places that access the brain through senses other than sight are particularly stimulating. Grass between the toes at Innocent Drinks, the sound of a planet gong at Procter & Gamble's clay street project or Bloomberg's multi-sensory information delivery all engage the brain in different ways, which in turn stimulates more creative thought. Finally, spaces that are devoid of stimuli can be just as useful to help people think differently. The Innovation Room at the LEGO Group's 'Idea House' and the clay street project's 'black box theatre' use this technique to great effect.

SPACES FOR REFLECTION

Reflective spaces promote the filtering of information into the brain, allowing it to make connections. Periods of intense focus coupled with time to relax and unwind set up the right conditions for a creative brain to problem-solve. Reflective spaces can create private moments, whether recharging in Google's water lounge or P&G's nap pods; or they can be relaxed, agenda-less breaks with friends in cosy corners, coffee stops or outdoors. Meditative-like states are induced by Bloomberg's colourful fish tanks and DreamWorks Animation's zigzag paths. Designed to deliberately slow people down, these devices create the headspace required for creative connections to be made. Spaces that provide areas of focus – such as Philips Design's creative turret, where future ideas are dreamt up, Sony Design's 'Sake Box' that overflows with ideas or Aardman's 'creative bolt-holes' – are invaluable areas of quiet contemplation.

SPACES FOR COLLABORATION

An essential part of any business, meeting spaces support the sharing of information and knowledge. But creative meeting spaces go further. Google's 'microkitchens' and Bloomberg's free pantry optimise chance liaisons (using food as a lure); Aardman Animation's nexus of walkways and Walt Disney Imagineering's 'Grafitti Hallway' force collisions; Virgin's themed rooms and random meeting generator encourage effective meetings. Large group collaboration spaces take the form of a lakeside amphitheatre at DreamWorks Animation and a café that transforms into a gig venue for Sony Music. Collaborative spaces energise people, put them at ease, make them feel connected with their colleagues and open them up to exploring ideas. Collaboration might also be in the form of iterative and continuous feedback; Innocents Drinks' centrally located development kitchen invites contributions from all, while T-Mobile's project room verandas manage informal and formal input. DreamWorks Animation's Halo suites and WDI's collaboration tool provide great creative examples of virtual collaborative spaces.

SPACES TO PLAY

Children at play are undeniably creative. When left with cardboard boxes or empty packaging they seem to invent endless possibilities. Many of the businesses in this book invite children into the workplace. Whether formally, as part of the creative process through Hasbro's 'Fun Lab' or the LEGO® company's co-creation sessions, or more casually through Nike or Electronic Arts' day-care facilities, these companies understand the creative value of seeing the world through the eyes of a child. Playful spaces elicit a lightness of being that opens up lines of communication between people, helps them to try new things and sometimes is just plain fun.

Play takes on many forms and is not only an essential part of learning and social development, it's also critical for creativity. There are a multitude of examples of playful environments in the featured businesses, each with a different tone and function. Active play is essential for letting off steam, expressing oneself physically and tapping into a kinaesthetic form of learning and communication. Oakley's motocross trail, quad bikes and military tank and the extensive sports and leisure facilities at Nike, Google and Electronic Arts form wonderful active playgrounds. Social play forms bonds with team-mates, developing trust and ease of communication, and is well represented at many of the companies who scatter games stations throughout workspaces. When seeking answers to a question, explorative play is the act of doing or making things to test and develop ideas. Tough security and hidden spaces such as Nike's Innovation Kitchen, Oakley's test labs and Dyson's biometric scanners encourage freedom behind closed doors. Role-play enables people to empathise with others. Ethnographic facilities at T-Mobile, simulated spaces at Philips Design and living room mock-ups at Sony Design help people to look at things from their users' perspectives.

Finally, playful spaces of course include a touch of humour. By simply injecting a playful energy into materials choices – such as Innocent Drinks' AstroTurf for carpet or the bold colours and jokey communication in Virgin's 'SCREW IT' – fun environments can lighten the load, lift spirits and reconnect people with their inner child.

HOW TO USE THIS BOOK

It's important to note that all the featured companies boast examples of each type of creative space, but cataloguing every detail is beyond the scope of this book. Rather, I have highlighted particularly strong, unique or interesting treatments of a type of space. For example, every company in this book has creative collaboration spaces, but DreamWorks Animation, Google and T-Mobile have noteworthy examples.

As you flip through the case studies, look out for examples of different types of creative space that are particularly relevant to you. You might want to read about a business that is in a similar industry to that which you're in, or you may find inspiration and neat solutions from unexpected sources. Feel free to browse, dip in and out or pinpoint a particular creative aspect or company that you're interested in. Alternatively, this book makes for a great doorstop/coffee coaster/fly-swatter.

Dotted throughout the book are metrics which illustrate business successes that are directly or partly attributed to the environment within which these creative people reside. These metrics span anything from market share to employee retention figures and are intended to give an indication of the past, recent and continued commitment to innovation of the companies who were generous enough to open up and share their worlds. The metrics are by no means exhaustive, but collectively they back up the argument that creative spaces impact these companies in many ways – not just the bottom line.

Don't be afraid to use the things you see in the book as they appear, but even better, be creative with what you find! Take the principles that you like and apply your own imagination and understanding of what works for you in your work environment. This book is a celebration of how great companies foster creativity *their* way and aims to provide inspiration for you to take the principles behind the ideas presented so you can do it *your* way.

Have fun!
For more information about Kursty Groves see:
www.iwishiworkedthere.com

AARDMAN ANIMATIONS LTD

AARDMAN HEADQUARTERS, BRISTOL, UK
ARCHITECT: ALEC FRENCH ARCHITECTS, 2009

AARDMAN Animations' new headquarters sits in the heart of Bristol's historic docklands, nestled among old warehouses and tucked alongside the rigging of Victorian steamship *SS Great Britain*. Close by, in the confines of a former banana ripening facility, a select team from this world-leading stop-motion animation studio painstakingly positions and repositions clay models, bringing to life their most famous of characters, Wallace & Gromit. The studio won its first Oscar® for *Creature Comforts*, charming animal creations voiced humourously by candid interviews with real people.

ABOVE **Wallace & Gromit, Aardman's most famous clay characters.**

OPPOSITE **Huge characters welcome visitors to the reception of Aardman Animations' headquarters.**

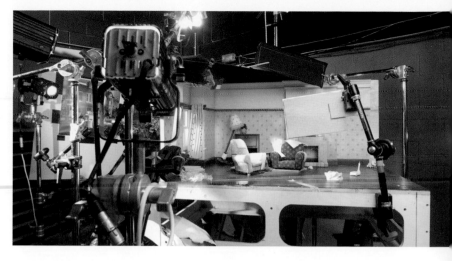

Aardman Animations took its first breath in 1976 when Peter Lord and David Sproxton created a simple clay character, Morph, which made its first appearance on television for children's programme *Take Hart*. Nick Park joined Aardman full-time in 1989 having met Peter and David when he was working at the National Film and Television School on his student film *A Grand Day Out*, Wallace & Gromit's first adventure. Their second adventure, and Aardman's first 30-minute film, *The Wrong Trousers*, won worldwide recognition and over 30 awards including an Oscar®. The studio has received seven Oscar® nominations, and has been awarded four. Aardman has continued to create award-winning short films, commercials and feature films. These include *Chicken Run*, *The Curse of the Were-Rabbit* which grossed $200 million at the box office, and the computer-generated *Flushed Away* in 2006.

Aardman's physical history can be traced through a number of buildings scattered across Bristol, ranging from spaces above shops to Georgian inns and even a Victorian veterinary pill factory. Their first real base was a 2,000-square-foot Victorian warehouse. Aardman made this building, chosen for its open space, workable by installing a mezzanine to house technical support and model-making, with simple offices below, leaving a void for studio space. In these early days, when only a handful of people were working on projects, this open approach provided the perfect creative conditions. 'Everyone was in audio distance of everyone; everyone knew what everyone else was doing,' David Sproxton, Executive Chairman, recalls. Over the years, Aardman found themselves taking on more projects, people and therefore space, with staff split across improvised studios and spread across the town. The distance meant fewer connections between studios on a regular basis and Aardman began to realise how quickly the communications they had in the early days were becoming fractured.

In 1991, Aardman bought a banana ripening plant on the site of former docklands; a building that provided 13,000 square feet of studio and space for their expanding office needs. As they grew out of this space they erected 6,000 square feet of Portakabins on-site to house a number of growing departments. The need for a larger studio space for the production of *Chicken Run* led to Aardman renting an 80,000-square-foot industrial warehouse across town, a studio still used today for large-scale productions and feature films.

ABOVE LEFT **An animator repositions a clay character during a commercial shoot.**

ABOVE **While the 'actors' take a break, a closed set is lit.**

OPPOSITE **Finishing touches are applied to a set in the Banana Warehouse.**

BELOW The creative team sit on an open space off the main studio in the Banana Warehouse, preparing artwork for an ongoing feature film.

THE BANANA WAREHOUSE

Once home to stowaway tarantulas, the Old Banana Warehouse had been left unused for several years before Aardman made it home to a crew of model-makers, set-builders, camera and lighting technicians, artists and producers. Its 25-foot-high ceilings and large spaces made this old building ideal for conversion into a film studio. The central core, where enormous refrigerators once slowly ripened bananas, became the studio void and an L-shape of offices hugged the external wall, housing the creative teams and production services. While the same basic layout remains today, the interiors have changed over the years: lightweight wooden walls divide up the studio space to accommodate the multiple set-ups used in stop-motion productions. Stepping in over cables and ducking beneath lights and rigging, one discovers caricature worlds in miniature that seem to hover against black curtains. Created with meticulous attention to detail, these charming models reflect the talent and

passion with which they've been made. The stop-motion process is supported by a model shop that handcrafts multiple mouthpieces and back-up characters, and which has, over time, learned what scale works best: too big and the set would require larger studios; too small and details are lost.

In a move to bring the key creative departments together under one roof, Aardman commissioned a new-build on the site where the Portakabins and car park once sat. This decision symbolised a commitment: the new building would not only tie up capital, it would also communicate a sense of permanence and belief in the future for the studio. Now, after more than 30 years in the business, Aardman has captured the energy and creative connections it had as a small group of animators and called on them to support and fuel a solid, world-leading entertainment business.

EMPLOYEE RETENTION FIGURES FOR AARDMAN

| <1 | 1-5 | 6-10 | 11-20 | >21 |

Years service

Adjacent to the old warehouse studio, the new headquarters stands proud, its contoured larch and sweet chestnut slats casting dramatic sundial shadows over its occupants: low and long in the afternoon, short and sharp in the morning. Bristol-based architects Alec French designed the building to minimise energy consumption as part of an overall sustainable approach, making use of significant extract ventilation and controlled daylight. A garden outside the canteen, a grassed roof accessible from the first floor and a roof terrace provide ample social spaces. To the rear, copper cladding weathers as the character of the building emerges.

An open, airy entrance presents a light-filled helter-skelter space of wooden walkways and stairs with skewed angles and a hand-crafted feel. Like old friends, oversized figures provide a warm welcome in reception, where scale models perch on glass-fronted meeting rooms that break into the triple-height atrium. The building funnels in, punctuated only by the bright colourful drums which denote junctions between the charming central staircase and wooden slatted balconies and bridges. The working areas are separated from the main space by shoulder- to above-head-height walls that offer varying degrees of privacy, yet allow visual connection from floors above. Each department is connected to the atrium and each other by uninterrupted lines of sight, developing a sense of unity reminiscent of early studio days. By co-locating what had tended to become rather disparate functions and skills, Aardman has created a powerful creative machine. With a new generation of audiences enjoying a more interactive relationship with the characters and stories, the company is able to take those characters, those worlds, that imagination and create new and exciting adventures for them through a variety of different channels. Specialists in online game design and web community managers have access to licensing experts and feature film animators; film editors and directors rub shoulders with scriptwriters and model-makers. This cross-fertilisation has bolstered the company's ability to retain consistency and control over the use and application of their characters, something that is essential to the success and growth of their brands. It has also had an energising effect on creativity; Dan Efergan, Online Creative Director, remarks: 'Now if I have an idea I can literally run upstairs and speak to someone – the amount that happens on the stairs and in the canteen is amazing.' The building has been arranged with meeting opportunities designed into the corridors and walkways for people to stop, connect and share their thoughts. 'People bump into each other and have those conversations that they wouldn't have formally,' says David Sproxton; 'the flow of traffic is encouraged to crash into each other.' With this in mind, the stairs are wide enough to pass by an impromptu meeting, while those colourful drums act as junctions where people can pause for longer spells.

ABOVE Visitors are swept into a light-filled triple-height reception atrium that tapers through to the canteen area at the rear. Natural materials, controlled daylight and ventilation make this a sustainable approach.

OPPOSITE Aardman's new headquarters in Bristol, UK.

LEFT A gently curved central stair spans freely between floors through the three-storey atrium, its crafted look reflecting Aardman's approach to animation. Large colourful drums punctuate high-flow areas to maximise opportunities for informal huddles.

RIGHT AND BELOW A connecting space.
A. Stairways and walkway junctions encourage spontaneous meetings and free exchange of ideas.
B. Teams are visually connected and have quick access to each other through a series of walkways.
C. Glass-fronted 'creative bolt-holes' that break into the main space offer quiet areas for focus yet retain a feeling of inclusion.

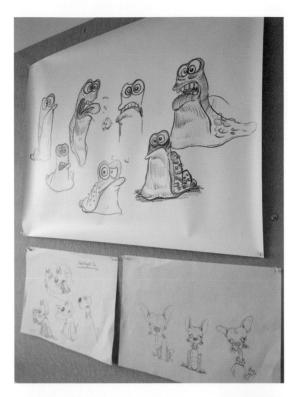

The new Aardman headquarters has the best of two worlds: combining an experience in the old warehouse spaces with the advantage of building from scratch. Over time, Aardman has come to realise that 'buildings are organic and need to flex with projects', as David Sproxton says. This philosophy manifests in the new building as enclosed meeting areas that are fixed in space and time, while the rest of the architecture is as flexible as possible. Very few walls in the building are structural; only a few go down to the concrete floor for soundproofing reasons, such as in the Cinema and Edit spaces for example. Power and communications are hidden beneath a suspended floor, and the remaining walls are reconfigurable, a lesson taken from the studio experiences; and while limited in number, the fixed spaces are essential to the success of the building, enclosed by glass and dotted throughout in various nooks and corners. These quiet, private spaces can be booked for anything from a 30-minute meeting to a six-month project and have found a life of their own. With such a vibrant, interactive, open environment they have become a haven for storywriters who need to access their thoughts and internal dialogue when creating. Merlin Crossingham, Creative Director of *Wallace & Gromit*, explains: 'Having the opportunity to come into a space like this is vital – these rooms are becoming creative bolt-holes rather than meeting rooms.'

From Peter and David's tabletop beginnings to blockbuster releases, Aardman has come a long way. This world-class studio now has a world-class environment that reflects its success, offering a wide-angled view of the business, with a tighter focus on continually refined and evolving processes. It's a big new space with room for growth, inspiring a sense of possibilities. Yet the charm, sense of humour and humility of Aardman's history pervades. As the team settles into this new space, they're beginning to make their mark. Artwork begins to spread across walls, personal spaces become busy with sketches and mementos, galvanised banisters show signs of polishing smooth, and the freshly painted walls welcome the odd thumbprint by the light switch. Reassuringly, Aardman's new space is not too perfect. They're scaling up, but they retain the all-important human touch.

LEFT ABOVE **Felt pin-boards share exploratory sketches.**

LEFT BELOW **Familiar figures provide a friendly presence – they work here too!**

RIGHT **Hand-crafted set models from feature films form characterful exhibits in the thoroughfares.**

Bloomberg

BLOOMBERG LP

731 LEXINGTON AVENUE, NEW YORK, USA
OFFICE DESIGN: STUDIOS ARCHITECTURE, 2005
BUILDING ARCHITECT: PELLI CLARKE PELLI ARCHITECTS (FORMERLY CESAR PELLI & ASSOCIATES)
INFORMATION DISPLAYS: PENTAGRAM

BLOOMBERG turns financial news on its head by revolutionising the way the world looks at commercial information. The same entrepreneurial spirit, clarity and passion for numbers that it applies to its business are also very much apparent in its workspaces. With over a third of international market share, Bloomberg is the world's leading financial news and data company; a media powerhouse, it has more than 10,500 employees in 137 offices around the world. Providing data, news and information such as analytics and equity trading platforms, data services, multimedia reports and real-time news through the colloquially-named Bloomberg Terminal, Bloomberg boasts over 280,000 subscribers to the BLOOMBERG PROFESSIONAL® service, which provides access to more than 3.6 million financial instruments, anytime from anywhere in the world.

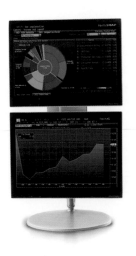

ABOVE The dual-screen Bloomberg terminal used by subscribers to the BLOOMBERG PROFESSIONAL® service.

OPPOSITE: 'The Link' is the main circulation area of Bloomberg's headquarters in New York where a free pantry, colourful information displays and access to email make it a hub.

As a wave of urban din crashes against the commercial district in Manhattan's midtown, visitors to Bloomberg's head office surface as flotsam in a cobbled courtyard, its cove-like shape offering welcome shelter. A 54-storey tower threads skywards through this moment of calm, cupped by a vast curved glass frontage. Beyond this lies the entrance where an unassuming corridor filled with the scent of a muscular yet sensual cedar sculpture stretches towards security. In the blink of an eye, visitor identification including your image is presented to you on a credit card. Embraced by this efficient yet reassuring welcome, you turn to the bank of lifts, silently contemplating what is yet to come.

A sudden blaze of energy and colour hits as you step out onto the sixth floor. High-speed data trapezes across a media wall split into four parallel displays. Colour-coded news and real-time information whiz overhead – a visual circus that delights and informs, yet nothing overwhelms. Designed to entice and intrigue, this place takes the chaos of the outside world and processes it, wiping your head clean and re-presenting information to you the way it should be: filtered and untangled. You have arrived at 'the Link', a curved glass bridge harbouring a criss-cross of escalators and stairs over three storeys, that connects two main towers and is home to an abundantly stocked free pantry. The buzz and energy of this space evokes 'a happy train station', says Dan Doctoroff, Bloomberg's president, remarking that 'if I stood here for two hours, I would see the majority of the people in the office pass through'. The lack of straight lines or walled corridors means that there is no singular, set direction for people to walk; instead there are numerous trails to be discovered. Open stairways and escalators maximise opportunities to bump into colleagues and share thoughts, a Brownian exchange as the flow of people jostle and collide, rarely taking the same path twice.

Light pours in on three sides, the curved white steel structure providing views past Bloomberg terminals set on chrome-topped counters out over the courtyard and back in the other side. A neutral palette of materials provides a visual datum: white walls, white terrazzo stairs, grey stone floors and carpet, steel, chrome and glass, which is brought to life with flashes of colour and Bloomberg's signature tropical fish.

LEFT A dramatic cove of composure: the curved shape of the building's facade creates a courtyard that welcomes visitors from Manhattan's busy commercial district.

OPPOSITE BELOW A disarmingly organic welcome to a high-tech company: a huge natural cedar sculpture by artist Ursula von Rydingsvard lines the muted hallway that leads beyond the check-in area.

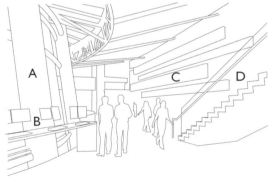

ABOVE The Link, a two-storey reception lobby, bustles with activity.

A. The curved glass structure maximises natural light entering the building.

B. Bloomberg terminals provide quick information access for visitors.

C. Colour-coded information whizzes across a large four-band LED display, designed by Pentagram.

D. Once on the sixth floor, the nexus of stairs and escalators is designed to maximise impromptu collisions.

LEFT Bloomberg's signature aquariums filled with tropical activity pose a calm reflection of employees busily darting to and fro.

RIGHT Rows of desks fitted with Bloomberg terminals echo the set-up of their customers' workplaces in an empathic gesture. Not even the CEO has a private office in this super-collaborative office.

FAR RIGHT A wireless, paperless office: meeting rooms act as transparent buffers between the open office and circulation areas.

BELOW Free food on tap all day at a Bloomberg pantry in the London office.

CLARITY AND OPENNESS

There is no reception desk in the Link; instead, members of the Analytics team, having received visitor information on a hand-held device, provide a face-to-face welcome for new arrivals. Not only is this a welcome personal touch, the lack of physical barriers is a feature that echoes throughout the organisation, revealing a transparent approach to business which is both unique and refreshing. For a company that deals with sensitive information, it would be convenient to keep things behind closed doors. But the commitment to open lines of communication is immediately in evidence through open-plan desking and walls of glass. There are no private offices at Bloomberg, rather 150 glass-walled conference rooms which can be used by all employees.

Mirroring their customers, Bloomberg employees sit shoulder-to-shoulder in an empathic gesture to the trading floor. While this arrangement fosters a sense of camaraderie among employees and a better understanding of their customers' situations, it brings with it the challenge of managing private conversations. The solution: easy access conference rooms encircle desk areas, forming a buffer between the backstage workspaces and the busy circulation spaces. Transparency is made possible at Bloomberg by its seamless technology. It's the ultimate paperless office where cables and clutter are replaced by hand-held devices and face-to-face interaction.

GLOBALLY CONNECTED – 24/7

Not only is information at Bloomberg shared quickly, it is shared globally and around the clock. Two meeting rooms, 'New York' and 'Tokyo', are connected via 24-hour video conferencing links and all are furnished with the ubiquitous Bloomberg terminal, where information is shared and traded and problems are solved every second of the day.

Whichever end of the line you're on, you know you're in a Bloomberg space – whether in the small and bijou Paris office or the lofty wharf-side San Francisco office, you'll encounter the same fish tanks, pantries stocked with local favourites, and those busy rows of Bloomberg desks. Bloomberg's New York office, like many of the newer ones, draws upon lessons learnt from the scores of Bloomberg buildings that have gone before. The most influential of buildings is the London office, whose redesign in 2001 incorporated an atrium that connects two buildings, with the pantry, central circulation and broadcasting facilities at the heart of the space.

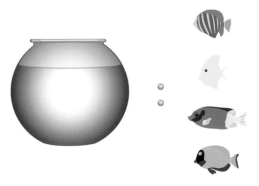

BLOOMBERG'S NEW YORK OFFICE HAS 150 GLASS CONFERENCE ROOMS, WITH A RATIO OF ONE CONFERENCE ROOM SEAT FOR EVERY FOUR EMPLOYEES.

ABOVE Room names refer to the locations of Bloomberg customers and a simple coding directory provides quick orientation.

LEFT Numbers are omnipresent at Bloomberg, from giant floor numbers to highly visible information displays.

OPPOSITE ABOVE At Bloomberg, information is presented in a visually dramatic way. Large lights above lifts beam green for up, red for down. A light installation displays Bloomberg offices around the world.

ABOVE The uplifting 100-foot-long light installation, *Sunrise* by Spencer Finch, brightens the lower-level training floor.

FAR LEFT Bloomberg's in-house two-storey TV studio.

LEFT A curved escalator provides a slow-motion descent from the sixth floor around a sculpture.

OPPOSITE A black chandelier flashes a poem in Morse code and a stocked koi pond at the base of the colour-lit stairs adds an unexpected note.

HARD FACTS, SOFT TOUCHES

There's a distinctive aural and visual identity that makes you feel at home at any Bloomberg location. Amid the hubbub of the public areas the occasional jingle sounds, gluing together conversation to create a familiar ambience, while colour and light is used at every opportunity. Above lift doors huge blocks of light beam green for 'up' and red for 'down', while each floor has a signature colour for easy navigation. Accent lighting on stairways glows red to the east, blue to the west; coloured glass meeting rooms tell you where you are and who's meeting who; and those vibrant information displays keep people up to date in an instant — green, a market is rising; red, it's an emerging one; purple for technology news; and blue lets you know that it's sunny in Damascus.

In a business that is built on delivering data, making quick-fire decisions and relaying time-critical information, one might expect the environment to be dominated by numbers, facts and figures. However, as the Bloomberg space sets out to stimulate the whole brain, a huge emphasis is also placed on sensorial aspects. The numbers are still there, but Pentagram has designed them into the fabric of the space, providing both navigational guidance and visual interest. Directories etched into meeting room walls provide quick orientation with shorthand numbers and digits indicating north, south, east or west and floor numbers. Even those flamboyant tropical fish serve a profound sensory purpose, as Tom Keene, Editor at Large for Bloomberg News Radio, reveals: 'Six years ago, I'd have said "how cute", but now, I realise that there's a deeper psychological link to our culture.' More than just interesting decoration, they mirror the activity of Bloomberg employees, and further, they provide an escape from the activity. Often you will find people slowing their pace as they pass, pausing, gazing, commenting on their favourite fish to a colleague who stops by.

Playing a significant role in the environment here, art stimulates tangential thought away from day-to-day business, and provides tangible connections with the outside world. It weaves moments of contemplation into this high-energy and fast-paced environment, while further opportunities to stop and take stock are built into the daily paths that people tread. A decadent black Venetian glass chandelier by Cerith Wyn Evans flashes a poem in Morse code, sharing an alternative method of information transfer; enormous vinyl figures by Julian Opie serve as a reminder that the business is about people; and a fluorescent lamp 'sunrise' by Spencer Finch offers inspiration in the training areas on the lower floors. An outdoor terrace is perfect for sipping a coffee and connecting with a friend; quiet, private rooms on the lower levels offer meditative respite, while a curved escalator gently guides people past the in-house television studio, spirals around a sculpture and delivers them thoughtfully to the next floor. In London, a 'tree' installation by Jump Studios over three floors offers a variety of casual meeting, breakout and contemplation areas.

ABOVE AND OPPOSITE An installation based on a tree over three floors in the London office by Jump Studios: lower-level meeting pods are formed in trunks; branches on the middle floor provide space for casual meetings; and lounging is encouraged on the top floor in the sculpted foam tree canopy.

A SPACE OF VALUES

Bloomberg was founded on the same values that New York's Mayor has taken with him to City Hall: Clarity, Communication, Empowerment and Entrepreneurship. 'If you can bring those values to life within the confines of one of the oldest municipal buildings in America and make them work, then of course the creation of a physical environment designed specifically to reflect and reinforce those values is even more powerful,' Dan Doctoroff says. When Bloomberg consolidated its headquarters from four different buildings in 1999, the transition was seen as an opportunity to create a space that would facilitate and enhance these values as well as the work function. The move enabled the execution of a three-dimensional manifestation of the company's DNA, where technology meets people meets design.

Bloomberg environments are full of thoughtful surprises designed to engage clients and employees alike, engulfing them in a sensory experience. 'Clarity' is far from an empty corporate directive or merely an overuse of glass, as in some organisations. Here, values are embodied through both the tangible and the intangible: from the abundance of natural light and transparent walls, floors and ceilings to the real-time information that is literally at your fingertips.

DREAMWORKS ANIMATION SKG

DREAMWORKS ANIMATION SKG, GLENDALE, CALIFORNIA, USA

GLENDALE CAMPUS
DESIGN ARCHITECT: STEVEN EHRLICH ARCHITECTS, 1998 | EXECUTIVE ARCHITECTS GENSLER ARCHITECTS
GENERAL CONTRACTOR: SWINERTON & WALBERG | LANDSCAPE ARCHITECT: SWA GROUP

LAKESIDE EXTENSION
DESIGN: GENSLER | CONSTRUCTION: TECTONICS | 3RD/2ND FLOORS – 2008 | 1ST/GROUND FLOORS – 2009

AMID the melting concrete of a Southern Californian warehouse estate, set against the hills north of Hollywood, sits the headquarters of DreamWorks Animation SKG (DWA). With its covered arched walkways, water features and hanging foliage, this lush Mediterranean-inspired retreat is where Jeffrey Katzenberg and a team of around 1,700 talented animators, artists, writers, technicians and producers come together to create hit animated movies such as *Madagascar*, Academy Award Nominee® *Kung Fu Panda*, and the Academy Award®-winning *Shrek*.

In 2004, DWA became the first animation company to produce and distribute two computer-generated animated features in a single year, including *Shrek 2*, one of the highest-grossing movies ever.

ABOVE Academy Award®-nominated *Kung Fu Panda* was a box office success in 2008, grossing over $600 million worldwide.

OPPOSITE DreamWorks Animation employees enjoy a game of table football on one of the many tables dotted around the 14-acre complex.

ABOVE DWA's *Boy in the Moon* topiary decorates the main piazza, where a water fountain acts as a focal point.

Beyond ivy-covered arches of the front gates to the DWA campus lies a vista of olive trees that cast dappled shadows over a nexus of pathways leading to a communal piazza and water fountain. Courtyards radiate from this central hub, connected by a constructed river that meanders through the 14 acres of landscaped grounds. Plasterwork is allowed to crack giving a rustic, comfortable feel to this man-made dream world. Perfectly imperfect, the environment echoes the working ethos, with acute attention to detail, colour and texture – a 'real' world that lures people out of the virtual ones they work so hard to create. With seven or eight projects going on at any one time, an essential part of the business is – as Dan Satterthwaite, Head of Human Resources, states – the 'bringing together [of] creative and technical people to create something new and different'.

Established in 1998 to accommodate 2D animators when hand drawing required as much light as possible, the complex was designed for individuals working in small offices with big windows. Traditional animation involves meticulously drawing frame after frame of artwork onto transparent cels, and the last thing any animator wants is to be disturbed halfway through a drawing, so their spaces were intentionally private. Over the past 10 years, computer-generated animation has become the medium of choice for blockbuster animated movies. Requiring a more collaborative process than traditional 2D animation, this new way of working placed more emphasis on the communal areas between offices, while windows were blocked up to provide better computer screen contrast. As a result of these environmental changes it then became essential for employees to take more frequent breaks away from their computers and to connect back to nature.

A recent 230,000-square-foot extension onto the 'Lakeside' building and a total refit of the remaining buildings reflect the different needs of the 3D animation business over traditional 2D practices. This new development has presented the opportunity to design completely new spaces that reflect and support the current processes and working behaviours, with new configurations that support more collaborative working. It's more open plan, but certainly not a sea of open space. Small bundles of artists, or 'four-packs', are clustered together in an area inhabited by about 30 people with tangential skills or who are working on similar projects. With autonomy over their work areas, these small groups are encouraged to configure their space as they like, creating lounge areas and decorating any way they wish.

ABOVE Through ivy-covered arches, the Mediterranean-inspired headquarters of DreamWorks Animation SKG is an oasis of creativity.

BELOW LEFT Homely common areas are just around the corner from work areas; sofas, fridges and dining-style tables line wide corridors.

BELOW RIGHT Interior lighting is kept intentionally low, to accommodate intense focus.

The layout of these interiors and the arrangement of the campus as a whole, has 'shifted from a more collegiate, spread out, suburban arrangement to one that is more like a city', explains Darren Osti, Head of Facilities. This move – from people separated by groves and courtyards, to a metropolitan layout with desks around a very public space in the interior – 'forces people to bounce off one another, then retreat to their huddles', says Osti. Not only does the space better accommodate both collaborative and individual working, allowing ideas sharing as well as private focus, it also supports the development of the tools and technology required to continue to make cutting-edge animated movies. With proprietary tools, creativity can be in the invention of new computer software as much as it can be a unique storyline or character design. The environment has played an important role in blending artistic and technical skills to support creation. A population of almost 200 technologists used to sit as a functional group. Now interspersed among the artists and animators, they can see how the animators use both their hardware and software on a daily basis and can interact with them moment-to-moment. An animator can suggest a new use or express a need while animating, and technologists can help with problems quickly. Interspersing technical and artistic talent, the creative, iterative journey is intensified and the whole process accelerated.

ABOVE Computer Graphics (CG) animators are arranged in 'four-packs' for increased collaborative working.

OPPOSITE A nexus of olive-tree-lined paths connects the five buildings on the site.

NUMBER OF FULL-TIME EMPLOYEES

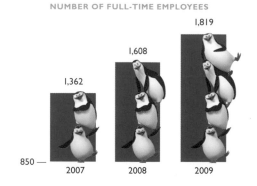

1,819

1,608

1,362

850 —

2007   2008   2009

INTENSE ARTISAN PROCESS SUSTAINED BY FORCED RELAXATION

While more collaborative than its 2D cousin, the intensity of current animation processes remains. At DWA, significant periods of concentrated, indoor and often solitary activity are counterbalanced by an environment that encourages people to relax and take a breath of fresh air.

The campus is intensely relaxing, with much work having gone into making the environment serene and calm. One of the main thoroughfares between buildings carves a zigzag path over a grassed hill, railings intentionally slowing people down to breathe the air, smell the bougainvillea and relax their minds. John Batter, Co-President of Production for Feature Animation, explains: 'We want people to slow down and take advantage of the surroundings – it allows them to think more creatively.' Those little moments of quiet are structured into the day. Water features scattered throughout the site disguise the sound of traffic passing on a freeway nearby. The effect is incredibly calming; mixed with the sound of wind through the trees, this creative white noise produces a relaxed brain state where ideas flow freely. 'It's such an intense creative endeavour, making these films – and the intensity can last for years – pounding out story ideas, figuring out how to make a fold in fabric look right, reviewing the shots until your eyes bleed,' says Kathy Altieri, Production Designer for *How To Train Your Dragon*; 'being able to walk outside for 15 minutes provides you with that release you need as a creative person to allow a solution to float to the surface.'

ABOVE The 147-seat silver-screen cinema with 3D viewing capability hosts movie-in-progress reviews and special events.

RIGHT A Halo video conferencing suite connects headquarters with studios in San Francisco and Bangalore, enabling creative reviews and ideas sharing across sites.

OPPOSITE The 'Lagoon' is a popular place for a quick break or casual meetings and doubles as an amphitheatre that can accommodate the whole company.

INDIVIDUALS AS A COLLECTIVE

Typical movie production involves many individual contributors who come together for a period of four to five years to work on a project. Over that time they bond to varying extents as a team, then disband at the end of the movie. At DWA, there is a more long-term view. Each movie begins with a small team who form the core, or what they call a 'hub'. As the movie develops, it requires more people, so the team grows as well as the space they occupy. Like a start-up company experiencing rapid growth, these teams swell from a small group of six to eight people to around 200 to 300 people, all working on the show at the same time.

As the team balloons, whole-team meetings and events become critical in maintaining an aligned vision and a vibrant team spirit. Themed parties are often held by the 'Lagoon', with frequent viewings in the fully equipped theatre to keep the entire team aware of the latest progression of the film. The personality of the movie is brought to life in these physical spaces through artwork, visual story development and rough scale mock-ups. Melissa Cobb, Producer of *Kung Fu Panda*, explains: 'Each movie has its own sub-culture – its own work style,

own attitude about themselves and their own goal for the movie.' The culture of the movie teams is grown and maintained for the duration of the project, and the spaces allow people to become totally immersed in the world of dragons, alien planets, kung fu or ogres.

Once their role on the movie has finished, each person is reassigned to the next project based on a complex combination of factors, which include their experience, their passion for a subject and their desire to develop new skills. This focus on career continuity and development is an important part of the culture at DWA.

ABOVE AND RIGHT
Forced relaxation:
A. Rippling water creates soothing sounds.
B. A zigzagging pathway is designed to deliberately slow down journeys, forcing contemplation and producing time to think.
C. Ponds and streams, stocked full of koi and home to baby ducks, provide much enjoyment for employees who stop to watch.

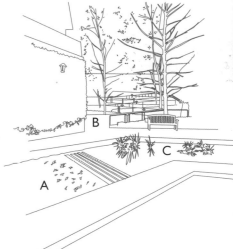

BELOW LEFT Semi-translucent dividers provide a canvas for fun scribbles.

BELOW RIGHT The central water fountain: a common intersection providing ample opportunities to connect and catch up with colleagues.

OPPOSITE An impromptu game of ping pong breaks out over lunch.

COMMUNITY

A strong sense of community can be found at DreamWorks Animation, where ideas are shared freely and people are nurtured. A key enabling structure that supports this is that people belong to two subcultures – cross-movie and cross-department – and they are encouraged to mix in a number of structured and casual ways. Every two weeks entire film crews get together and share what they're working on – no matter how unfinished the work might be. This is encouraged as much with technicians as it is with artists, and getting people over the fear of sharing progress early on opens up lines of communication: 'the campus is built this way for a reason, it's a relaxing environment. There's probably nothing scarier than putting your idea out there,' says John Batter; 'you want the environment to put people at ease in how they share their ideas and we reinforce that throughout the campus.'

The organisation of workspaces also mitigates that fear. An environment of learning and nurture resounds with a mentoring system as well as mixed learning, where young and old learn together in related and tangential classes ranging from photography to sculpture to life drawing. A recent graduate might find themselves taking a class with an Art Director or Head of Facilities. The community reaches beyond the hedged walls of the Glendale campus with its Halo video conferencing suites. Connecting three sites and two time zones, this state-of-the-art technology places PDI/DreamWorks in San Francisco and a new office in Bangalore virtually on each other's doorstep and allows inter-site creative meetings to be held at any time of the day.

DreamWorks Animation SKG has created a mini world of its own, where its people seamlessly switch from intense creation to deep relaxation, where technology is balanced with nature and where forced collisions and chance encounters keep their creative spirit alive.

dyson

DYSON

HEADQUARTERS, MALMESBURY, UK
MOVED TO SITE IN 1993
EXTENSION ARCHITECT: WILKINSON EYRE, 1998

AN undulating steel wave, mounted on a glazed facade, floats above buttercup-laced meadows in England's West Country. This 'quirk' in the quintessentially British countryside, which sits on the outskirts of the idyllic market town of Malmesbury in Wiltshire, is home to a very English success story. The man behind the business, James Dyson, is a home-grown inventor who through creative thinking, sheer dogged determination and hard work, created an original product that beat the big boys and redefined appliances as we know them. The headquarters' distinct steel structure, designed by Wilkinson Eyre and Dyson's old friend the structural engineer Tony Hunt, can be viewed as a proud expression of the great tradition of engineering and entrepreneurship from which Dyson originates.

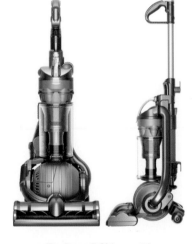

ABOVE The Dyson DC24: an upright vacuum cleaner that features patented technology for maintained suction and better manoeuvrability.

OPPOSITE A crystalline cube topped with a lightweight canopy, which contrasts with the 'sheds' either side, defines the entrance to the Dyson facility.

It took James Dyson five years and 5,127 prototypes to come up with his first bagless vacuum cleaner which, rejected by British manufacturers, started selling in Japan in 1986. Dyson's Dual Cyclone™ technology was developed to solve the problem that conventional vacuum cleaners have picking up dirt, as they lose suction when their bags become clogged up with debris. In his usual style of seeking solutions from unexpected sources, Dyson was inspired by a debris extractor in a sawmill which used centrifugal force to expel waste. Reasoning that a vacuum cleaner could separate dust on a smaller scale, James set to work on making rough prototypes from cardboard and duct tape to create the world's first cleaner which didn't need a bag or filter.

Dyson Ltd was founded on the curiosity of one man, driving the company to success through his iron will, and with the original product undergoing countless revisions. Today that spirit is evident in its 300 or so design engineers, who continually seek solutions to everyday problems. Although the first Dual Cyclone™ that went to market far outperformed its closest competitors, the company hasn't stopped there. Instead it has continued to develop cyclone technology, as well as coming up with new innovations such as the energy-efficient Dyson digital motor and highly manouevrable Ball™ technology. Additionally, Dyson has expanded its product range to include hand-held cleaners, the world's first dual-drum contra-rotating washing machine, a bladeless fan and the Airblade™, the world's fastest, most hygienic hand dryer which is 80 per cent more energy efficient than conventional warm air dryers.

OPPOSITE An elegant use of glass reveals the engineered structure of the building, a reflection of a unique feature of Dyson's vacuum cleaners: the transparent dust collection bin.

BELOW An undulating waveform roof 'floats' above the trees and disguises the bulk of the factory, which was the building's original function.

Dyson is now a truly global brand, with the business expanding to 2,400 employees and selling its machines in some 47 countries. It remains a privately owned company, with a turnover in excess of a billion dollars.

Dyson's headquarters was built on the site of a former lighting factory in 1993 at a time when Dyson was the fastest-growing company in the UK. The original building was created with expansion in mind to include an on-site factory along with the research and development and operating functions of the company. The manufacturing function was moved to Malaysia in 2002 and today the building is home to an expanded R&D operation and customer service centre.

On arrival, visitors are drawn towards a shining glass cube beneath a lightweight tented canopy. This crystalline structure connects existing and new buildings, and communicates an early expression of the Dyson ethos, the company's personality and a sense of what it holds dear. The clean, functional, highly engineered structure echoes Dyson's style of products and a fascination shared by Dyson design engineers with how things work. Through the glass reception doors, into the belly of this huge transparent machine, a limited palette of materials reinforces a sense of precision and attention to detail. A reverent display of bright, futuristic-looking Dyson products, individually spot lit and preserved behind glass, greets visitors with the clear message that this is a place that is all about invention.

Beyond thumb-print recognition security, Dyson's 'engineers' roam free. A mix of disciplines ranging from generalists to specialists, and including concept designers, industrial designers, motor engineers, acoustic engineers and even microbiologists, are grouped together in one big, uninterrupted space. Now known as 'the Cathedral', this building used to house the laundry appliance factory and spans over 330 feet. Interspersed between rows of side-by-side desking, sound-absorbent screens developed by Dyson engineers use layers of impregnated rubber, acoustic foam and transparent fabric to absorb the sound frequencies of human speech.

Punctuating the rows are 'Concept Areas' furnished with circular review tables, where teams gather around drawings to discuss and develop design ideas. Simple and functional, these unimposing glass-topped tables elegantly reveal the structure of the table and provide a great surface for drawing on. One of the glass tables has recently been converted by engineers to become a light-box table. Practical solutions such as this run throughout Dyson, with many designed and executed by Dyson engineers themselves. The huge expanse of open space encourages an active approach to communication, with people getting up to go and speak to a colleague face-to-face rather than blind behind computer interfaces.

A recurring theme for Dyson's creative engineers is the desire to make things work better. Whether born out of frustration with an existing product or finding a new

OPPOSITE 'The Cathedral' is one large space where the entire team of around 300 'engineers' research, design and develop new technologies and products.

RIGHT Dyson engineers brainstorm product developments with James Dyson, who challenges ideas and supports the philosophy of failing often in the pursuit of success.

BELOW Dyson engineers have over 20 laboratories and workshops in close proximity, including rapid prototyping facilities, a microbiology lab and model-making shops.

application for an interesting technology, this varied mix of designers, developers and researchers is focused on generating, developing and prototyping new ideas. An integral part of Dyson's philosophy is that failure is essential for innovation. This belief resonates through James Dyson's story and is reflected in the prototypes that are proudly displayed in the workspaces. For some, the 5,127 prototypes it took Dyson to get his first product to market might sound tedious. To Dyson himself, failures are fascinating: 'Each failure, the 5,126 failures taught me so much. Success teaches you nothing. Failures teach you everything. Making mistakes is the most important thing you can do.'

This resolve to find the right solution through the physical testing of prototypes is supported by the environment with over 20 labs, workshops and – as Paul Dawson, Senior Design Engineer, puts it – 'lots of space to design and develop, test and tinker'. There's quick access to 'dirty' workshops, where design engineers make foam or cardboard models of product parts – 'anything to make ideas real, try things out, test them, break them, learn from them and develop them further,' explains Dawson.

A 'hands-on, everyone gets involved' ethos is encouraged by an expectation to do a myriad of jobs and is bolstered by frequent contact with James Dyson, who spends time daily in the research, design and development space challenging engineers to think about things differently. Getting their hands dirty means learning about the

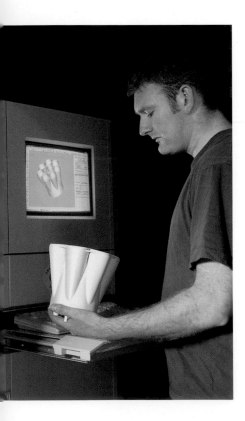

whole creation process, all the while learning to take risks, make mistakes and use frustration as a fuel for creativity and solving problems. Such is this intense level of involvement in the entire process that Dyson engineers are able to create a product from scratch.

Situated off the research, design and development space, beyond the acoustic testing chamber, a cyclone visualisation lab and the dust pick-up chamber, is the 'user course': an area mocked up to resemble a living room, kitchen and bathroom that is used for testing out new ideas, for understanding ergonomics and how users interact with appliances in their homes. With easy access to these spaces, engineers can quickly develop ideas in a contextual setting. The on-site facilities at Dyson that support the entire creation process – from concept to prototype to production-ready design to testing and refinement to post-production improvements – have promoted a feeling of self-reliance. While Dyson engineers don't deliberately isolate themselves, their head-down focus on getting things to work creates a sense that if something doesn't exist, they have everything they need to create it right there. As the company has grown, it has continued to invest half of its profits back into harnessing new ideas – the return on which includes an impressive 820 patents to Dyson's name.

Dyson's group of creative engineers are a curious bunch. Being based deep in the countryside, far from the cosmopolitan hub of London, does not deter them from connecting with the world around. Actively seeking feedback from customers via the on-site call centre, by accompanying field service engineers to home visits or by

ABOVE Testing facilities include acoustic chambers, laser flow visualisation facilities and robotic test rigs.

AVERAGE WORLDWIDE SALES (£ MILLIONS)

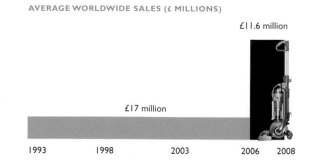

£11.6 million

£17 million

| 1993 | 1998 | 2003 | 2006 | 2008 |

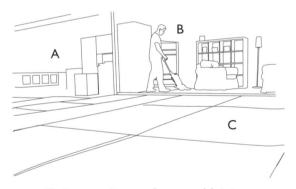

ABOVE The 'user course' is a space for contextual designing:
A. Areas are set up to simulate a kitchen, living room and bedroom.
B. Designers trial production models for usability and new prototypes to further develop ideas.
C. A range of different floor coverings.

OPPOSITE 39 life-size figures made from reclaimed copper water tanks by British sculptor Paul Burke decorate the exterior courtyard. Their construction encourages curious Dyson engineers to 'peer into their inner workings'.

demonstrating products in-store, Dyson engineers create opportunities to learn more about the way their products are used by consumers. The inquisitive nature of Dyson engineers' minds extends to looking to the outside world for inspiration: as Paul Dawson observes, 'quite often looking at new technologies or different ways of doing things can spark off ideas for new applications of those technologies and new ideas'. An innate characteristic of a Dyson engineer is the propensity to take things apart (often pilfering objects from around the house for reverse engineering). Regular 'product autopsies', where teams pull apart products to understand how things are being developed and made, are not intended to encourage copying, but rather to stimulate those curious brains to think about interesting applications.

At times when Dyson engineers get stuck or need a quiet space to focus, often a change of environment helps – whether sitting in the mock living room, going for lunch outside in the courtyard or strolling along a nature trail that circles the building,

Dyson has created an environment that supports the many iterations that are involved in fully evolving and developing a product by providing the space and tools that allow people to try things, test them, break them, and learn from the experience. By placing everything at people's fingertips and maintaining a physical focus, Dyson's engineers have developed a sense of self-reliance that fuels their desire to find unique solutions themselves.

ELECTRONIC ARTS

EA, REDWOOD SHORES, CALIFORNIA, USA
INTERIOR ARCHITECT: GENSLER, 2002
EXTERIOR ARCHITECT: SKIDMORE, OWINGS & MERRILL, 2002

TWENTY miles south of San Franciscan fog, the headquarters of Electronic Arts (EA) sits on the sunny side of the bay where year round the temperature never falls below 15 degrees Celsius. Since its inception in 1982, EA has been developing, publishing, marketing and distributing video games. Its most successful products are sports games published under its EA Sports label, games based on popular movie licences such as *Harry Potter* and games from long-running franchises like *Need for Speed, Medal of Honor* and *The Sims.*

Built through several acquisitions, the company also publishes games that have been conceived or developed by others. This and partnerships with companies such as Hasbro make up a rich and varied portfolio of games that extend movie experiences beyond the screen, enhance social networking and appeal to the strategist within us.

ABOVE **Tiger Woods PGA Tour is one of Electronic Arts' games under the EA Sports label.**

OPPOSITE **Areas positioned off main thoroughfares offer inviting places to stop to meet or play a game.**

Electronic Arts Redwood Shores (EARS) is the site of the company headquarters, where, based on a on a 'city-state' model, each of three 'labels' – EA Sports, EA Games, EA Play – operates as its own business, making its own decisions without the distractions of a larger, centrally governed organisation. Set on a 27-acre open business park with some shared outdoor space, the four concrete and glass constructions, designed by architecture giant Gensler, form a campus that surrounds a full-size soccer pitch. Some 2,000 people occupy three of these buildings; the fourth building known as 'The Commons' houses a huge canteen, games room, basketball court and a 6,300-square-foot free gymnasium.

Upon entering the dark, cavernous lobby of the main building, eyes take a few moments to adjust and are quickly drawn toward the flickering colours of an oversize screen that hovers over the reception desk. High above, theatre rigging, coloured spotlights and trailers from recent game releases punctuate the darkness. Funnelling visitors in past back-lit posters and gaming booths, this dramatic entrance has movie-theatre connotations, communicating the fact that EA is not just in the business of gaming, but in the business of entertainment. At once you get the feeling that these guys know how to create a sense of drama and that the environment (both physical and virtual) is important here.

The scene beyond secure doors delivers a shock to the senses. The dark lobby opens out into a huge communal space with comfortable seating, friendly chatter and the aroma of freshly brewed coffee. Natural light pours in through four-storey high windows, engulfing retinas and forcing pupils to contract. As they adjust, eyes settle on tropical palms, a gallery displaying employee artwork and an open gaming annexe filled with both digital and analogue games. Within a few moments the EA experience unfolds around you. It's clear that this company is all about gaming and that interactive entertainment is

ABOVE Spot-lit gaming booths invite visitors to play while they wait.

RIGHT A full-sized soccer field sits at the centre of the campus, forming the backdrop for lunchtime football matches, summer barbecues and product launch parties.

OPPOSITE The main entrance of Electronic Arts at Redwood Shores. Trailers and advertisements for the latest game releases bombard those who enter with flashes of colour and light.

part and parcel of what they do.

At EA, the role of the environment in helping to ensure a positive work/life balance is taken very seriously, with the Vice President of Facilities and Real Estate, Curt Wilhelm, reporting directly to the Executive Vice President of Human Resources, and a facilities team that is second to none. 'The physical spaces and the way that the teams interact with them have become a crucial element in maintaining high performance and retaining talented game designers, developers and artists,' explains Curt. In order to continually produce blockbusting games in a market where agile, young, independent game companies have all the kudos, EA rewards and engages its people through freedom and an autonomous environment, the design of which is specifically aimed at enhancing and maximising creativity. Created by the facilities team, who borrowed the behaviour patterns and creative proclivities of the most successful teams at headquarters, these principles have been replicated across 24 EA studios globally.

ABOVE Artwork decorates the walls, corridors and meeting spaces, immersing teams in the details of the games they are creating.

ABOVE LEFT A life-size game character guards its creators' territory.

OPPOSITE The light-filled four-storey atrium – with coffee shop, soft seating, artwork on display and games stations – is one of the most successful collaboration spaces on the campus.

2004

2007

FOLLOWING A FOCUS ON LONG-TERM PROJECT PLANNING, COMPENSATION AND COMMUNICATION WITH EMPLOYEES OVER THREE YEARS, AN INTERNAL EA EMPLOYEE SURVEY IN DECEMBER 2007 SHOWED A 13% INCREASE IN EMPLOYEE MORALE.

ABOVE The ultimate cube: one game designer has blocked in his workspace to form a complete box!
A. Large boards propped atop cubicle walls create a low ceiling with only a small hole left open to the outside world.
B. Lit predominantly by their computer screens, game designers can lose themselves in virtual worlds.

ABOVE LEFT Game creative teams are arranged in 'neighbourhoods' that change visibly depending on the game theme and genre.

OPPOSITE Creative team workspaces are designed with privacy in mind, rather than flow of traffic. A solution to the common problem of people getting lost: lampposts point the direction of game teams.

LIGHT AND DARK

The arrival experience at EA refracts throughout the campus in many different ways. The interplay between light, dark and space is exploited to provide areas of individual focus, team collaboration, casual socialising and personal refreshment. Continuous movement from dark spaces to light spaces – such as lobby to atrium or work desk to football pitch – focuses and refocuses attention, punctuating the day and challenging or calming the senses. Like a jolt of coffee or a soothing bath, EA uses lighting and spatial contrasts to control and facilitate emotional state, encouraging different types of creative activity. Large, open spaces with lots of natural light such as the atrium or cafeteria, with easy circulation and high flow of traffic, maximise socialising and casual encounters. Pausing here to browse artwork or grab a coffee, employees can take a seat and have a kick-about ideas session where the sky is the limit, the huge ceiling height drawing the eye up, opening minds and clearing heads.

By contrast, individual creative workspaces are typically dark, enclosed and often with limited access. There are no formal lighting systems in these areas; employees are instead allowed to dictate the light levels themselves. So you can go from one area that is furnished with fairy lights and hanging lanterns to another where designers have blocked themselves into a pitch black 'work cave' fashioned from foam board, illuminated only by

BELOW This turf labyrinth is based on medieval mazes used for private meditation and acts as a physical reminder that creativity can happen anywhere.

BELOW RIGHT This full-size professional basketball court is a popular perk, and has been host to several NBA-player games.

a computer screen. This is a unique atmosphere of committed, focused creativity, with employees lost for hours on end in their own virtual worlds. These hard-working passionate people are encouraged to play whenever possible since they are trusted to get the work done.

Here, the creative spaces are not open-plan, nor are they easy to flow through or access, because an important part of the creative endeavour of the game developers is focus. The warren-like layout is formed into cube communities, each visually representing the game area its inhabitants are working on through lighting, colour, artwork and other objects of stimulus – such as decapitated heads and alien gunge for Dead Space™, designer furniture for MySims™ and brightly coloured cartoon characters for children's games. The tone of the team spaces changes as you pass through: each territory has its own distinct personality. This provides a sense of community and camaraderie as well as the opportunity to bring the game to life in their physical surroundings. While the occasional street sign points the way, the locals don't want lots of people traipsing through their intense work zones. However, the isolation of these workspaces is countered by team spaces that are designed to connect people in both structured and ad hoc ways; project 'war' rooms for sharing ideas, screening rooms

for progressing and refining game development, and more casual communal areas that entice people away from their desks to play games together.

Surprisingly, this is not a place for pallid couch potatoes. There is a healthy, outdoors feel to the place, with alfresco meetings, barbecues on the lawn, and lunchtime soccer games all part of daily life at EA; the understanding of the value of play is implicit. People here play more than just computer games and it is supported in every way imaginable – from fairground games to air hockey, SCRABBLE®, Wii™, basketball or pool – you name it; the passion for games is across the board.

At EA, these competitive yet friendly, hard-working yet fun people enjoy the challenge and release that comes with the intensity of work and the support of their environment. Caring and considerate, this is a place where sustainability issues and low-impact activities reflect the concerns of a young, educated and responsible eco-aware community, and where facilities are focused on giving employees everything they need at arm's length – well, maybe at a stroll's length.

BELOW **Opportunities to play games – old or new, physical or mental, digital or analogue – exist at every turn on the campus.**

Google

Did you know ... ?
... that a Google employee is called a 'Googler', a new employee at Google is called a 'Noogler' and that a Googler from the Zurich office is called a 'Zoogler'?!

GOOGLE

GOOGLE, MOUNTAIN VIEW, CALIFORNIA, USA
BUILDING 43 (MAIN BUILDING): DESIGN: CLIVE WILKINSON ARCHITECTS AND GOOGLE IN-HOUSE TEAM, 2004
BUILDINGS 40, 41 & 42: GOOGLE IN-HOUSE TEAM

GOOGLE, ZURICH, SWITZERLAND
DESIGN: CAMENZIND EVOLUTION AND GOOGLE IN-HOUSE TEAM, 2008

GOOGLE, NEW YORK, USA
DESIGN: HLW INTERNATIONAL LLP AND GOOGLE IN-HOUSE TEAM, 2006

GOOGLE is the world's most used Internet search tool and one of the most recognised brands. In just 10 years, the business has grown from a little-known group of Stanford students to a global company of over 20,000 employees cited by *Fortune* magazine several years running as one of the best places to work. Its mission is to 'organise the world's information and make it universally accessible and useful', and to this end, Google's ubiquitous search engine has been joined by a number of innovative online tools such as Google Earth and Street View.

One of the few original dot-coms to survive the 2001 technology crash, Google has continued to exhibit mammoth growth and release new-to-the-world innovation year on year. This success is testament to visionary leaders, smart business practice and a genuine belief in the value of the employee.

ABOVE Google Earth is a virtual globe that shows the topography of landscapes and cityscapes in 3D. A Googler invented its flight navigation feature in his spare time.

OPPOSITE Reclaimed Antarctic expedition igloos make fun yet inexpensive meeting pods in Google's Zurich office.

Google's headquarters (nicknamed the Googleplex) is based in Mountain View, California – about 35 miles south-east of the heart of San Francisco, and close to the buzz of other technology companies and web-based start-ups. Its main campus comprises four buildings, with dozens of other spaces scattered over a tree-lined business park. With creative knowledge application at the heart of what they do, it has served Google well to use the physical environment to reinforce its culture, facilitate creative endeavour, and appreciate its employees in subtle and cost-effective ways.

Despite the business's incredible growth, the culture here remains as strong, relevant and fun as it was when there were only a handful of university students, and a truly college campus feel is maintained throughout the offices globally, regardless of physical orientation or building design. The bicycles, handmade posters and suit-free atmosphere developed in Mountain View have been preserved and adapted at other Google offices – because the shared attitude is that 'it's all about learning'. This approach is supported by an environment that was established upon a set of basic principles and standards, yet has the flexibility to accommodate individual-, team- and location-based personalisation.

OPPOSITE A full-scale replica of Tyrannosaurus Rex hangs out with Googlers on the Mountain View lawn.

BELOW LEFT Google's New York office is home to 2,000 Googlers.

BELOW Google's world headquarters in Mountain View, California comprises four buildings on the main campus, with dozens of other buildings on the peripheral campus.

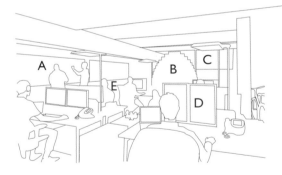

ABOVE The basic ingredients of a Google environment (shown here at the Zurich office):

A. Whiteboards everywhere – because ideas can happen anywhere.

B. Casual meeting spots (they're not all egg-shaped).

C. Local task lighting for personal control.

D. While workstations are standard, from day one Googlers choose their own software, operating systems and hardware – even the monitor orientation.

E. An efficient mode of transport.

THE BASICS

Ever entrepreneurial, Google has maintained a great physical environment without lavish expense, and as a result a sense of fun and passion runs through the business. This is achieved by attending to basic human needs first, making sure that technology fully supports the employees and then adding a unique twist. By prioritising in this way, Google provides a level of comfort – physical and psychological – and once these fundamental needs are addressed, people feel ready and able to focus on their work. At its very core, Google is committed to ensuring that people are healthy and happy. Provision of clean air, natural light, food and laundry facilities are some of the ways that this philosophy manifests itself.

Indoor air quality is of foremost importance because for Google the physical well-being of its people comes before anything else. The environmental controls at Google's main complex consist of commercial-grade air handlers with enhanced filtration of the air that is introduced to the office environments. What would be considered a normal pre-filter and bag filter assembly has been modified and offers 30 per cent better indoor

air quality than would be experienced by use of normal industry filtration methods.

Natural light is maximised by arranging workspaces in glass cubes around the internal perimeter of buildings, which provides an energy-saving double-glazing effect and in turn maximises interior floor space for communal areas and meeting rooms. This standardised configuration of workspaces also creates an atmosphere reminiscent of the early days: autonomous teams are clustered in small groups of three or four people, each with their own responsibilities, which fosters and fuels the entrepreneurial spirit that pervades Google.

ABOVE LEFT At the New York office, Manhattan skyline wallpaper brightens up what could be a dull internal hallway. With the office spanning an entire city block, scooters have become the way to get around.

ABOVE At the Zurich office, found ski gondolas repurposed with a Swiss theme make great cubbies for private phone calls and quiet work.

BELOW In Mountain View's main building, stand-alone yurts insulated with recycled denim form unique team spaces.

FOOD, GLORIOUS FOOD

Since the Googleplex was not established in a downtown location, there was a need to provide food on site; but, in true Google style, they did it differently. Rather than hiring external caterers or providing vending machines filled with junk food and bad-tasting coffee, they were one of the first large-scale companies to provide free food served up by passionate chefs. Furthermore, fulfilling their own unwritten rule of thumb which states that no Googler should ever be more than 150 feet away from food, 'microkitchens' were conceived, where employees help themselves to a wide variety of snacks. Always with health and performance in mind, less wholesome items are kept behind the glass of a solitary vending machine on the Mountain View campus, still available to all, but coming with a health tax: Googlers pay for food containing hydrogenated fat and lots of sugar and salt. Google doesn't view its food facilities as mere feeding stations or refuelling stops, but rather as great places for new and continued discussion and having ideas.

BELOW **A beach-style 'tech stop' at the Zurich office. These IT support stations are found dotted around Google offices.**

OPPOSITE **New York: wherever there's an opportunity for people to meet and relax, there's an opportunity for ideas. This floor-to-ceiling graffiti wall in the New York office encourages Googlers to make their mark.**

Ideas are the currency of this business and at Google there's a deep understanding that they are not confined to specific times or places. In fact, it's expected that a good idea will often develop over a cup of coffee, over lunch or on beanbags on the lawn. Nothing communicates this better than the plentiful whiteboards scattered throughout Google spaces – from team areas to coffee lounges, and especially next to the pool tables! These are ever-present reminders that shared thinking is valued and that ideas can happen anywhere, even in the corridors.

Anticipating that ideas surface when people meet serendipitously, Google offers a multitude of opportunities to connect and collide away from traditional workspaces. An important part of the Google set-up is the inclusion of many different destinations to draw people off the treadmill and encourage them to stay a while. Games by the microkitchens, cappuccino machines that require a PhD and a good 10 minutes to operate, and bar stools in the 'tech stops' are just a few examples of the many different devices used to encourage people to slow down and connect in informal ways.

FEBRUARY 2009 – GOOGLE TRANSLATE CATERS FOR 98% OF LANGUAGES READ BY INTERNET USERS

2% not included

HIGH-SPEED COMMUNICATIONS

At Google the culture of sharing information freely, easily and quickly has fostered a very open, energetic environment. Meetings that would take hours elsewhere are frequently little more than a conversation in the lunch queue. Even the lavatories provide an opportunity to communicate, and cubicles are littered with posters displaying web links to 'Fix-it' forums (where Googlers are invited to combine their brains on unsolved problems) – because here saving time is of the essence. With millions of Google users, shaving a fraction of a second off every search query has a profound effect on the quality and experience of the product, and this philosophy recurs in the physical space in a myriad of ways. From scooters in Manhattan to zip-lines in California and firemen's poles in Zurich, taking seconds off the time it takes to get from one end of the complex to the other might seem trivial, but when multiplied by the hundreds of trips taken by thousands of employees every day the effect is, in the words of co-founder Larry Page, 'significant'. These natural problem solvers thrive on finding neat and frugal solutions to life's challenges. Sofas brought in from home, an old English telephone box 'won' on eBay, chairs from flea markets – these simple solutions have become an essential facet of Google's quirky and eclectic style and offer a great opportunity to assert local identity.

GOOGLY PRINCIPLES, LOCAL FLAVOUR

With offices and centres of engineering all over the world, maintaining a sense of identity is important for preserving the Google culture. Visit more than one location and you begin to appreciate that there is a balance to be maintained between a strong company identity and encouraging expressions of local flavour. The same fundamental principles are shared across any Google office globally: individual-to-team space ratio, common areas and number of meeting rooms as well as a few staples such as the microkitchens, tech stops and lava lamps in the lobby, but there's also a different Googly imprint to every office. Two great examples are the Zurich and New York offices.

With over 500 people, Zurich boasts the largest population of Google engineers outside the USA and, as one of the newest spaces in the Google family, has benefited from experiments and learning from other offices. Located in an old brewery, a complete refit enabled the best of Google working environments to be put into implementation. With 100 meeting spaces to furnish on a budget, the in-house team had the freedom to break away from the standard glass cubes, instead fashioning 'huddle spaces' from reclaimed ski gondolas, refurbished Antarctic expedition igloos and egg-shaped dens, each decorated according to different themes that correspond with different working floors.

7 Soups, Stews & Chowders

G Global

Q Quick Salads & Sand...

Meanwhile New York is the largest Google office after Mountain View, spans an entire block in Manhattan's Chelsea district and is home to around 2,000 Googlers. Here, microkitchens look more like funky loft apartments, scooters replace those Mountain View bicycles and its floor plan echoes the Manhattan street layout. By having a standard approach to the way the company operates – learning what works and continually building on that – Google saves on having to reinvent and redesign the basic workspace. Importantly, the company has a solution for keeping entrepreneurial energy alive, while leaving room for local teams to cast their own image and personality on the spaces. This is empowerment and individuality at work, all at once.

ABOVE The familiar sight of a free cafeteria at Google is flavoured with a splash of New York: an industrial warehouse feel and subway-inspired signage.

OPPOSITE Microkitchens are destinations that have been deliberately built into daily Google life. Each one has a different feel and is stocked with different food preferences, so people are encouraged to visit different spaces throughout their working week. The unwritten rule, that no Googler is ever more then 150 feet away from food, means that there is an abundance of opportunities to stop, refuel and casually connect with co-workers.

SERIOUS WITHOUT A SUIT

With a spaceship, slides, igloos and firemen's poles, Google's office spaces sound more like a themed adventure park than the working environment of a global brand. Yet while Google has developed a reputation for goofy-sounding offices, what lies beneath the bright colours, lava lamps and yoga balls is a deep understanding of the drivers behind creative thinkers and how the environment can play a huge role in making challenging work fun. By developing and nurturing a relaxed, playful and fun atmosphere, more profound, human connections are created among people, reducing the fear factor and ensuring good work gets done. At Google the culture and internal practices often evolve as a result of environmental needs, not the other way around. A slide isn't a childish gimmick, it is an efficient way of descending from floor to floor. Coloured exercise balls are good for your posture, cheap and fun.

OPPOSITE **The library on the top floor of the Zurich office.**

BELOW LEFT **Two endless pools in the Mountain View campus: all the benefits of a swimming pool on-site, without the cost, space or maintenance issues of a full-size pool.**

BELOW **In Zurich, the well-being of Googlers is maintained through subsidised massage, beauty treatments, on-site doctors and even a laundry.**

ABOVE LEFT AND RIGHT Time is of the essence: Google's time-saving solutions include community bicycles in Mountain View, scooters in New York and a fire pole in Zurich.

OPPOSITE Zurich's Water Lounge: a place to 'chillax'. No BlackBerries®, phones or talking allowed. Googlers recline in a bath of foam blocks, chaise longue or massage chair, and emerge revived, refreshed and raring to go.

AN ENVIRONMENT OF APPRECIATION

Google is proud of its environment and protective of its 'perks', but the things the company provides for its people over and above standard office facilities may be seen by critics as traps to entice hard workers to work longer and even harder. Dan Ratner, a mechanical engineer on the Street View team, refutes this when he says: 'Good organic food is functional. If you're healthier you're happier and if you're happy you think better.'

Swimming pools, gyms, games rooms, subsidised massage and hairdressing, volleyball courts, wifi-connected shuttle buses, 20 per cent time to work on projects of personal interest; they are all smart solutions to the everyday problems that people face when trying to be at their best. The soft stuff is not seen as soft, but part of how to run a successful business. The 'work hard, play hard' mantra is woven throughout every second at Google. The freedom, trust and respect that is afforded to people generates in turn the desire to give great work back. And when people feel appreciated, you do not get standard, cookie-cutter ideas, but individual, personal touches such as the flight simulator for Google Earth. These are smart people, being treated in a smart way. And when you treat people well, they give their best back.

HASBRO

HEADQUARTERS, PAWTUCKET, RHODE ISLAND, USA

BUILDING 1011
ARCHITECT: LINDSAY BOUTROS-GHALI

BUILDING 1027
ARCHITECT: KUWABARA PAYNE MCKENNA BLUMBERG ARCHITECTS
INTERIOR DESIGN: SUSSMAN/PREJZA

NESTLED in a quiet leafy corner of New England sit the two unassuming, single-storey buildings that make up Hasbro headquarters. Cheerily guarded by a 6-foot statue of MR. POTATO HEAD™, the red-brick walls and manicured hedges provide a neat homely exterior concealing a world of creative chaos and boisterous activity. As if being one of the largest toy and game companies in the world weren't enough, Hasbro strives to be more than just another manufacturer; the company is in the business of inspiring imaginations, creating experiences and telling stories that make the world smile. Hasbro's portfolio includes a mix of home-grown and licensed brands, reaching across a wide range of audiences and its interests – from boys' toys to family board games, life-size animatronics to collectors' figurines.

ABOVE Some of Hasbro's brands include the CRANIUM® board game, PLAYSKOOL infant toys and I-DOG® animatronic pets.

OPPOSITE The 'Fun Lab' is Hasbro's kid-testing zone. Here, new toy concepts are put to the test by children who are invited to play under supervision.

ABOVE Hasbro's corporate headquarters is home to some of the most recognised toys and games in the world, such as MR. POTATO HEAD™.

ABOVE RIGHT Heavy curtains and warning chevrons mark the entrance to Hasbro's 'Innovation Hallway', an area dedicated to the next generation of products.

OPPOSITE A vibrant display of some of the toys and games that have made Hasbro famous.

In 1923, two brothers – Henry and Helal Hassenfeld – founded Hassenfeld Brothers, a textile remnant company in Providence, Rhode Island, which later expanded to produce pencil boxes and school supplies and then doctor and nurse kits, its earliest toys. Hassenfeld Brothers' first major hit was MR. POTATO HEAD™ in 1952. Shortening its name to Hasbro Industries in 1968, the business grew through a combination of internal product development, acquisitions and character licences. Hasbro, Inc. now employs over 6,000 people and is the parent company of several brands, including PARKER BROTHERS, PLAYSKOOL, MILTON BRADLEY and TONKA, who contribute to a significant portfolio of toys and games such as MONOPOLY™, TRIVIAL PURSUIT™, PLAY-DOH™, and the TRANSFORMERS™ and STAR WARS™ action figures.

Hasbro launches 2,500 new items and produces 10,000 packages per year and with such a diverse range of brands and categories, it could be difficult to know which ideas to prioritise. In 2001, a critical decision was made to focus on developing existing products and creating new brands they can control, rather than invest in licences they don't. This simple strategy has allowed Hasbro staff to channel their creative energies internally and has had a profound effect on the ideas that result. 'Focusing on fewer properties has had a freeing effect, giving ideas room to breathe,' says Duncan Billing, Global Chief Development Officer. 'If you try to do too many ideas then, by definition, none of them has the space to grow big.'

ABOVE Designers create their own caves of inspiration, surrounding themselves with objects and artefacts, images and materials that help them to develop their ideas.

OPPOSITE Main Street, the arterial connector of Hasbro's Toys campus, has become an important working space used for internal communication and to build excitement.

KIDS AT HEART

It's no surprise that the people at Hasbro love what they do – and that they're all kids at heart. If they weren't, they wouldn't be able to connect with their consumers or delight them generation after generation as they do. But it's the way that this passion for fun and games manifests itself physically in their surroundings and how people behave within that environment that allows them to channel that playful energy into productive creative work.

The reception in this converted factory explodes with colour and fun, with window-lined corridors displaying its famous games and toys. Many of these iconic products are highly collectible and worth huge sums, with Swarovski-crystal-encrusted MR. and MRS. POTATO HEADs™ and one of the first ever MONOPOLY™ prototypes, handmade by the inventor and lovingly preserved behind glass. These are artefacts with a significant place in popular culture, and are imbued with deep meaning that evokes highly emotional memories for many.

Turn the corner and duck below flying NERF™ darts as you enter Main Street, the artery through the headquarters and the pulse of the business. Oversized TRANSFORMERS™, a life-sized Han Solo encased in carbonite and gigantic MONOPOLY™ pieces flank a thoroughfare that makes adults feel as though they've shrunk and become kids again. This is where big events are regularly held, product and movie launches celebrated – it's a place of much excitement.

One of the many ways that creative energy is generated at Hasbro is through the 'Innovation Hallway', a converted walkway used to display soon-to-market products. Branching off from Main Street and concealed behind dramatic dark curtains, access is limited to employees and select retail buyers. Realistic product models and pack prototypes provide an on-site glimpse into the next generation of toy and game innovation, creating a sense of urgency around ideas soon to be hitting the shelves. With this ability to test new product and pack ideas in a replicated store setting, problem solving opportunities are presented, retailers engaged early in the process, and momentum is generated, which accelerates launch cycles. While not a substitute for industry toy fairs, the Innovation Hallway is a fantastic use of the environment to draw people in and get them excited about what's coming next. Main Street and the Innovation Hallway are wonderful examples of Hasbro's ability to inject fun into any space. These circulation areas, which were effectively dead space, have become important working spaces for the company, brought to life through frequently changing features that are used to communicate with staff and visitors.

REVENUE $ BILLIONS
IN 2008 REVENUES GREW
FOR THE FOURTH
CONSECUTIVE YEAR.

2.8 3.1 2.9 3.0 3.1 3.8 4.0

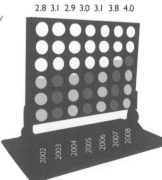

2002 2003 2004 2005 2006 2007 2008

FUN LAB

Decorated like a kindergarten with child-sized tables and chairs, beanbags, colourful rugs, and just about any toy or game a kid could ever imagine, the 'Fun Lab' is an essential tool for Hasbro. Behind a one-way mirrored window, designers and researchers observe children doing what they do best – play. Watching and listening to the kids interact with toys and each other connects Hasbro teams with their primary consumer. The Fun Lab is a place where new ideas arise, existing ideas get better and insights about how children play are uncovered. It is an essential part of the creation process, as Alan Gong, Senior Vice President of Global Games Design, explains: 'The best ideas at Hasbro are the ones that are grounded in insights, getting to the heart of the emotional connections that our consumers have with their toys.' The inclusion of this on-site facility is not only a cost-effective and controllable solution, it brings consumers closer to designers and integrates them into the process. 'This helps us to always remember who we're creating for,' says Brian Chapman, Senior Vice President and Head of Design and Development; 'it's super valuable.'

DESIGN AND MAKE

Behind bright red doors, stretching out beneath the 58,000-square-foot open expanse of the self-supporting saw-tooth ceiling, lies a labyrinth of cubbyholes filled with toys, inspiring artefacts and stuff to explore. It's in these 'creative caves' that Hasbro designers and developers live, separated by 7-foot-6-inch-high drywalls that offer pin-up space and shelving filled with toy parts, mechanisms, rough models and an incredible range of stimuli. Teams are physically arranged around a focal point by category: pre-school, girls' toys, boys' toys. Within these zones, the personality of each brand is manifested in the items that these folk surround themselves with. To the untrained eye, this maze of gadgets and gizmos might seem messy, but to the occupants it is a source of inspiration and a reminder of achievements.

The collector mentality that accompanies Hasbro's die-hard toy and games enthusiasts is evident here as complete collections of toys, row upon row of special-edition figurines and seasonal derivatives line shelves in work areas. People surround themselves with details and artefacts from STAR WARS™ to TRANSFORMERS™, THE LITTLEST PET SHOP® to I-DOG® body parts. Each work den is further personalised to suit working habits because, as Brian Chapman explains, 'customising your own space is important for people to get into a creative mindset, so creative chaos is inevitable. Having things at your fingertips that inspire you – throwing colours on the wall – whatever helps.'

ABOVE AND RIGHT An I-DOG® designer in her workspace.

A. A variety of storage solutions for artefacts and inspiration.

B. An exercise ball used as a chair.

C. Digital drawing tablets allow for quick ideas creation, sharing and remote review.

D. Prototypes, models and production copies of I-DOGs® in various stages of development.

OPPOSITE TOP Digital taxidermist heaven: row upon row of animal prototypes surround robotics engineers.

OPPOSITE MIDDLE Hand-painted finishing touches are applied to colour perfection, setting the benchmark palette for manufacturers.

OPPOSITE BOTTOM At Hasbro, people are encouraged to think in their own way, whether modelling in clay at their desk, sketching by hand or electronically.

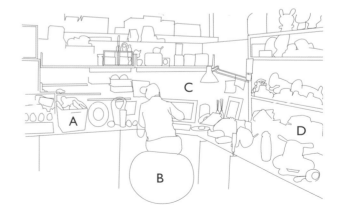

ABOVE The Hasbro Production Studio has full production and post-production capability. Here, the team can create the advertising, web-content, packaging and audio requirements for their toys and games.

This includes the way in which individuals explore ideas too. Most designers are equipped with Cintiq digital drawing tablets – lightweight flat screens that allow the user to draw directly onto them – which have revolutionised the business through quick ideas sharing and development globally. Alternatively some prefer to think more physically in three dimensions, sculpting ideas in clay and using materials samples and toy parts for inspiration. 'Everyone is encouraged to think in their own way. Whether through a drawing, a model, or even singing a song – whatever it takes to have an idea,' says Brian Chapman.

Located in close proximity to the design area is the model shop, where ideas can be roughed out quickly. All figures are sculpted internally, mostly by eye and hand, while digital scanning, haptic 'virtual' sculpting and 3D printing stations are scattered throughout the space. Working closely and collaboratively with designers, Hasbro engineers are able to take new ideas and make them function. These are creative engineers, who are open to trying out 'crazy stuff', yet grounded in the practicalities of mechanical, electronic and manufacturing reality, which means that time and effort is not wasted chasing ideas that

wouldn't work. Ideas are by no means limited to the designers: entire brands having been created by the engineering team at Hasbro – the first commercial interactive animatronic toy FURBY™ and later BUTTERSCOTCH PONY™ were created and fine-tuned here.

    All of this high-energy fun, like too much fizzy-pop, can get a little overwhelming at times so there are places to relax – without a moulded plastic shape in sight. Adjacent to the main building, in the centre of the corporate headquarters building, rests a Zen-like dome of serenity surrounded by Hasbro's senior executives. At the flick of a switch, electrochromic windows toggle between opaque for privacy, and transparent for more light. A place for quiet contemplation, the absence of toy-related stimuli clears the mind while the energising, grounding influence of trees, natural sunlight and waterfalls soothes over-stimulated eyes, ears and minds. Of course the silence in this oasis of calm has been broken on occasion by a test launch of a new GI JOE™ boat – 'to see if it floats'.

TOP AND ABOVE With a fully functioning professional-grade TV Studio, Sound Recording Suite and Photography Studio, Hasbro is able to create the entire toy experience surrounding a toy or game.

ABOVE **The circular atrium that connects senior management offices provides a stark contrast to the crowded and colourful hustle and bustle of the Design and Development offices.**

OPPOSITE **A girls' toy designer surrounds herself with toys, objects and images that serve as inspiration for the baby-animal-inspired range of products she creates.**

BUILDING EXPERIENCES

Storytelling is an important part of Hasbro's design process as it allows the team to form deeper connections with their audience. The products that they create are wrapped in stories to heighten experience and spark imagination; a plastic sword wielded by a sculptor in the model shop is not just a sword, but the sword of Argon, that has slain 1,000 dragons. 'We make the stories and support the communications behind and around the toys and games, bringing them to life,' says Terry Scott, Senior Vice President and Head of Creative Services.

One of the most recent additions to the site is the Hasbro Creative Production Studios. Nicknamed 'Cake Mix Studios', it is a video-production studio within the company whose name derives from an analogy used to describe how Hasbro integrates toys and games with movies, television, mobile phones and the Internet. The idea for the studio grew out of the early planning for the *TRANSFORMERS*™ movie, as Hasbro workers produced small vignettes to illustrate their ideas for the motion picture. The two-storey annexe, opened in January 2008, is equipped with a state-of-the-art television studio, photography studios and audio recording facilities. In one year it typically shoots over 100 commercials and film clips, 300 sizzle reels (short video presentations that communicate new ideas and generate internal excitement), web and electronic game content along with around 6,000 packages plus 1,500 exclusives of toys and games. Working closely with the engineering and project teams, marketing and design, this creative facility enables Hasbro to bring to life the whole experience surrounding a toy or game, as they have all the ingredients and capabilities to do it themselves.

MAKING THE WORLD SMILE

Hasbro is in the business of fun, but they take that responsibility seriously. Their workspaces are equipped to allow a sense of individual focus yet encourage collaborative efforts to build not just the toy or the game, but the entire experience surrounding it. By bringing the capability in-house, providing the facilities, tools and space to both design and make, Hasbro's teams have the freedom to create new product experiences that make the world smile.

INNOCENT DRINKS

FRUIT TOWERS, SHEPHERD'S BUSH, LONDON, UK
DESIGN: IN-HOUSE DESIGN TEAM, 2000
MEZZANINE AND FINAL EXTENSION: IN-HOUSE TEAM WITH HELP FROM JUMP STUDIOS, 2007

INNOCENT Drinks is a UK-based fruit smoothie company, founded in 1999 by three college friends, Adam Balon, Richard Reed and Jon Wright. These Cambridge graduates were only a few years out of college, working for other firms and with no previous experience of running their own company. Their business idea was conceived on a weekend snowboarding trip, based on their perception that most people find it difficult to get their daily intake of vitamins and minerals from natural ingredients. The trio set out to create honest drinks with fresh fruit and 'no nasties' and spent their evenings and weekends developing a plan and product, before 'test marketing' with £500 worth of fruit. Innocent now employs around 240 people, with offices in London, Paris, Hamburg, Copenhagen, Dublin, Stockholm and Salzburg.

ABOVE Innocent smoothies are made with fresh fruit and 'no nasties'.

OPPOSITE Innocent enjoys a relaxed yet buzzy atmosphere. Picnic benches and AstroTurf flooring encourage employees to kick off their shoes.

SHALL I COMPARE THEE TO A SUMMER'S DAY?

ABOVE The outdoor space at Innocent feels like a country garden. Adorned with straw bales and bunting, the quiet shaded area provides a peaceful meeting spot.

From the car park of Fruit Towers, the headquarters of 'Europe's favourite little juice company' (an aspiration voiced in co-founder Reed's vision statement) looks just like any other unit on a humble industrial estate in a semi-urban borough of West London. With a concrete driveway, brick exterior and a pitched tin roof, visitors could be excused for thinking that they'd arrived at an underused storage facility. The only hint that things might be different here are the grass-covered and cow-disguised vans parked out front. Step through the main doors, and you're greeted by friendly faces, shaded beneath huge parasols on a field of AstroTurf that stretches throughout the 18,000-square-foot building.

Innocent does 'open-plan' well. You'll not see private offices for the founders or the senior management team. Nor will you see miles and miles of desk space or workers' cubes. What you will see is a large, open communal space, furnished with picnic benches, booths, table football and an archetypal English red telephone box. The space is large enough for the whole company to gather at once – for example at their Monday morning meetings, where business updates are shared, or for more casual affairs, like the annual 'Summer Lunch Series', when free food is served once a week by local vendors.

A mezzanine breaks the view, creating an upper work area that, while separated, remains very much a part of the main space. Alcoves and small rooms peel away to the sides, while suspended basket chairs offer space for quiet moments and noontime naps. At the heart of the main space is a large, open, family kitchen where food and drink are on tap and most employees pass daily. Jenny Wilson, Environment Manager, observes: 'The kitchen is always the hub of the house, isn't it?' Positioned adjacent to the communal 'chill-out' space, it is indeed a hive of activity throughout the day.

The buzz of 200 people in this space gives it the feel of an English village fair, while countless potted trees and picnic benches complete the notion that you're outside on a sunny summer's day. The fake turf teases you to kick your shoes off, and looking around you can see many who have succumbed to the notion. Tucked away to the rear there is a lovely tree-lined, outdoor 'beer garden' area comprising 300 feet of shaded gravel with (of course) more picnic tables: perfect for summer events, impromptu meetings or simply catching a breath of fresh air.

ABOVE Innocent's headquarters, Fruit Towers is, in fact, six single-storey units knocked together.

BELOW LEFT Innocent's cow vans come complete with horns, eyelashes, udders and a 'Moo' button.

BELOW The large, communal 'chill-out' space is equipped with movable picnic benches that provide the flexibility to create space for full company meetings.

ORGANICALLY GROWN

When the business grew from one unit to six, the team worked hard to preserve the personality and attitude that was intrinsic in the early working environment. In the beginning, there were just four or five people hanging out in one big space; sourcing the right fruit, designing the packaging, persuading supermarkets and stores to distribute their product and communicating with their drinkers about why their drinks were so good. As the business continued to evolve, the founders realised that working in close proximity to each other had a positive side effect on their culture, allowing them to share and solve problems together while contributing equally to the growing business. There was no master plan for the space – rather an intuitive sense of what worked for the brand, the culture and the business. This understanding guided the in-house team, as Jenny recalls: 'We knew we had a great recipe for what was working and just re-created it.' In this most organic way, the fundamental principles of Innocent's space were born: keep things open, mix people up and keep them close to each other, but give them space to escape, and you'll keep the natural, creative buzz alive.

ABOVE A twice-yearly 'desk shuffle' supports the mixing of seating, providing a fresh perspective of the business and an opportunity to make new friends (and find out how they like their tea).

OPPOSITE The reception area at Innocent Drinks instantly communicates the personality of the company: a friendly place that makes honest fruit drinks.

BELOW Innocent employees sit in a mixed arrangement to enhance the flow of communication. One of the few teams that permanently sit together is IT, so people know where to go if their laptop breaks down.

MIXING IT UP

At Innocent your desk neighbour could be from Marketing, Product Development, Design, Finance, People or Operations. Every six months, there's a 'desk shuffle' – where the majority of people pack up their belongings and go to sit somewhere else, in a new part of the building, next to new people. There are only a few departments that cluster together permanently for practical reasons. Originally everyone was arranged randomly, but people soon found that not knowing where to get assistance with a computer problem was an issue, so IT was moved to a central location, with visible signs to let people know where to go for help.

This periodic reboot of people's working spaces keeps the employee perspective of the business fresh, reinforcing how one fits into the business equation, while encouraging greater communication and bringing 'innocent' eyes to a problem or issue. 'The insight I get from sitting next to someone who does a different job to me – not even from talking to them all day, just having their stuff around and seeing what they're doing – grounds me in what it is we're here to do, what it's all about,' Dan Germain, Head of Creative, observes.

ABOVE Personal desk space is deliberately limited to encourage people to use the more open, casual spaces for meetings.

ABOVE RIGHT Cosy, secluded nooks provide quiet respite from the buzz of the main space.

SHARE OF THE UK SMOOTHIE MARKET (JUNE 2009)

82% Innocent Drinks   Competitors

CUDDLE UP CLOSE

As the company continues to grow and space becomes a premium, Innocent doesn't scrimp on the communal areas that are so important to the company's culture — instead people just bunch up closer in their desk areas. The sense of camaraderie, that employees are all in this together, is palpable. Sharing these spaces provides a high degree of visibility, which in turn generates a healthy sense of competition. Employees are inspired by the standards they see around them, and are easily able to give feedback, challenge and contribute, as Karen Callaghan, Head of People, explains: 'Sitting next to people from other teams gives you easy access to new perspectives, great brains and you can't help but get involved and learn about stuff that you wouldn't ordinarily.'

Such physical closeness generates a viral buzz, as people's energy bounces off one another and spreads throughout the company. This high level of energy is sustained and tempered by the many pockets of quiet spaces and private nooks that are dotted about the building, giving people the chance to take their laptop to a sofa or a hanging chair for a change of scene, to seek new inspiration or retreat for some peace and quiet.

SPACE TO CONTRIBUTE

All of Innocent's creativity comes from within. All their products are invented, designed, made and tested in the Development Kitchen, which is located slap-bang in the middle of the building. Glass walls separate this controlled environment from the office space, which ensures its activities are highly visible and invites contribution and feedback. This generates shared anticipation around new product development, and since no one has the exclusive right to ideas, anyone can wander in and say, 'My mum puts cinnamon in hers – have you tried that?' Packaging, advertising and graphic design are also all developed in-house, and yet there are no formal brainstorms. The collaborative nature of Innocent's culture and the general accessibility to all employees means that ideas are born and built all day, every day.

The environment itself continues to benefit from employee suggestion and implementation; a behaviour that is key to this virtuous circle. When people feel free to add their own ideas to the space, their willingness to contribute to the business follows through. Dan Germain recognises this when he says: 'Creative environments are a sum of the people in them. Everything you see here was made or designed or thought of and executed by a person in this building.'

ABOVE Hanging basket chairs add to the choice of places to escape to and think.

LEFT The informal culture at Innocent encourages a no-nonsense approach to business. No suits, just straight talking.

Contribution is also elicited from consumers. Innocent 'drinkers' have an open invitation to visit Fruit Towers: the warm, friendly and approachable internal nature at Innocent is applied to external friends too. With Fruit Towers located 'off the beaten track, you know the people who make the effort to come and visit do care,' says Dan Germain. This inclusive approach encourages customers to provide feedback and ideas around Innocent's products, all of which are prominently displayed.

INFORMAL AND INEXPENSIVE

Nothing in the Innocent offices costs much, the majority of the environment budget is spent on the basic fabric of the building and the focus is on keeping things simple, natural, open and light. Everything else is informal and inexpensive; 'not swish, much to the frustration of architects who saw this space and thought, "Fabulous, let's really go to town with this,"' Jenny Wilson recalls.

This attitude is reminiscent of the original entrepreneurial spirit that continues to thrive and encourages a sense of resourcefulness. It gets people thinking about how they can create a fun environment in new and different ways, rather than heading straight to the office equipment store, where everything is uniform and expensive. The location of the business reflects the importance of keeping things practical and inexpensive. It is not located in an area of high property prices, and doesn't compromise on the amount and quality of space. 'Ours is the ugliest building in the world from the outside,' remarks Germain, 'but inside it's perfect – we've been able to grow and spread.'

OPPOSITE AND BELOW LEFT The Development Kitchen is where new smoothies are invented. Made visible behind glass and located in the centre of Fruit Towers, people are encouraged to contribute their ideas for new flavours.

BELOW Innocent 'drinkers' receive an open invitation to visit Fruit Towers, and the evidence of their passion for the brand and product is proudly displayed.

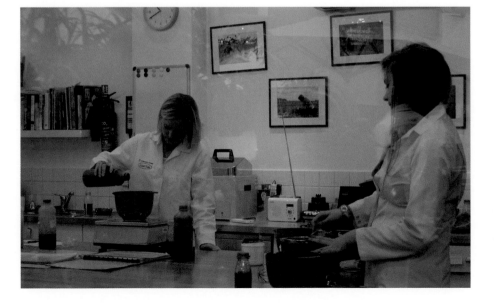

CHEEKY LITTLE TOUCHES

A distinct aspect of Innocent's brand is its tongue-in-cheek sense of humour and no-nonsense approach to business that has not only helped to create a unique product in the marketplace, but also supports a creative culture where employees are free to have fun and share ideas, no matter how crazy they may seem. 'We add little touches to our products and our packaging to show drinkers there's a human being behind them,' says Germain. Refreshing, natural and straight-talking, with nice, cheeky little surprises. As a consumer, that's what you experience with the Innocent product and brand. This is reflected so well in the physical environment, through some of the fun choices for the materials and details, the use of fun language in communications, and the continuous contribution from the people who work at Fruit Towers to keep things 'Innocent'.

TOP The human tone of language employed by Innocent on its packaging and external communications is reflected internally. Baby pictures of employees surround Innocent values.

ABOVE 'The Big Knit': a portion of profits from every drink sold with a hand-knitted smoothie hat is donated to Age Concern to support older people in the winter months.

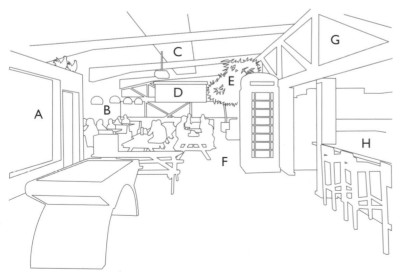

ABOVE Innocent's main space and the 'hub' of the building:
A. Shed-like rooms provide private meeting areas that are visually connected to the main space with glass doors and windows.
B. Diner-style booths allow for impromptu or casual meetings.
C. Skylights throughout the buildings provide ample natural light.
D. A large drop-down screen for company meetings or watching big events.
E. Potted trees are dotted throughout the space.
F. A red telephone box doubles up as an Internet station for guests and a quiet place for private calls.
G. The mezzanine level provides additional desk space without compromising the open-plan feel.
H. The large, accessible family-style kitchen at the heart of the building is always alive with conversation.

Johnson & Johnson

JOHNSON & JOHNSON

GLOBAL STRATEGIC DESIGN OFFICE, NEW YORK, USA
DESIGN: LALIRE MARCH ARCHITECTS LLC – 16TH FLOOR: JUNE 2007; 14TH FLOOR: DECEMBER 2008

Did you know ... ?
... that BAND-AID®
Brand Adhesive Bandages
were invented in 1920 by
a Johnson & Johnson
employee who found a way
to quickly tend to his
accident-prone wife?

RISING above the ordinary-looking commercial buildings that line New York's Hudson River, the Starrett-Lehigh Building, with its curved sweep of banded windows, presents an awesome sight. This landmark building, completed in 1932, spans an entire city block just north of Chelsea Pier, and was originally constructed as a rail-freight warehouse. Now occupied by some of the hippest names in media, fashion, entertainment and business, it is the chosen home for Johnson & Johnson's relatively new team of designers, media planners and the NEUTROGENA® cosmetics brand.

This Fortune 500 company has become a household name in medications, first-aid supplies and consumer products. With operations in more than 57 countries, its well-known brands include BAND-AID® Brand Adhesive Bandages, JOHNSON'S® Baby products, and LISTERINE® mouthwash, sold in more than 175 countries.

ABOVE JOHNSON'S® Baby products, like other J&J products, have built a strong reputation for the company over its 120-year existence.

OPPOSITE A rescued sign from a closed-down factory.

In 1886, Johnson & Johnson was founded by three brothers in Brunswick, New Jersey, on the novel idea of providing medical professionals with wound dressings to better treat their patients. New Brunswick remains the site of its headquarters and is known as 'the Healthcare City'. Johnson & Johnson has a rich history of developing new products and services that aim to 'advance the health and well-being of people'. Far from an empty promise, Johnson & Johnson has a respected reputation with a strong sense of ethics, guided by a credo that acts as the company's 'moral compass', informing decisions that have seen the business continue to flourish more than 120 years after its inception.

Establishing the Global Strategic Design Office was a big undertaking for Johnson & Johnson. It meant a positive shift in the value of design as well as accepting that in order to attract and retain the right talent, they'd have to venture into the bright lights of Manhattan. While New York is only 31 miles from New Brunswick, it turns out that it was the right move to make: bringing all of the management of Johnson & Johnson's design work in-house has enabled them to establish a vision, create a consistent approach to design, facilitate the clarification of what these hugely diverse brands mean and – believe it or not – save money.

The driving force behind this change is Chris Hacker. As Johnson & Johnson's Chief Design Officer, he reports directly to Consumer Group Worldwide Chairman Colleen Goggins. He says: 'Part of my coming to Johnson & Johnson was to be able to direct and design new ways of seeing these classic and iconic brands.' So when deciding to set up

TOP An Art Deco-style former rail freight building in New York's Chelsea is home to Johnson & Johnson's Global Strategic Design Office.

ABOVE A glossy red marque wrapped around a concrete corner reveals a confident and playful treatment of the company logo.

RIGHT A living piece of art capturing J&J's history, growing over time with new additions.

OPPOSITE Johnson & Johnson's credo is etched into glass atop a stack of reclaimed wood. Miniature packs form an explosive display across a facing wall.

ABOVE An external corridor follows ribbon windows as they wrap around the space, providing views of the Hudson River and the Manhattan skyline. The curves of the building create natural places to meet.

an internal resource, Hacker knew he had to find a space that 'shouts creativity and innovation'. One of the things that attracted Hacker to the challenge of creating this new movement within Johnson & Johnson was the ethical values of the company: 'The company is all about taking care of people and the planet and everything in the process,' says Hacker – which was something that clicked with the ex-Senior Vice President of Marketing and Design at Aveda, 'so we worked hard to make our design approach and our physical space as sustainable as it can be,' he says.

The reception to the 26,000-square-foot facility is on the uppermost of two floors. Opposite the lift and straddling a grey wall edge, the glossy red script of the Johnson & Johnson logo strikes out against the rough texture of raw concrete slabs; a beautiful play on light, shade, texture and colour, and a confident treatment of the company's famous marque. An early indicator of what is to come, this celebration of industrial materials and form communicates to visitors that here is a space where designers think and are not afraid to try new things.

Through glass doors, the spacious reception is dominated by huge 8-foot letters – an old factory sign that Hacker rescued from a decommissioned facility. The timely salvaging of the vintage sign reflects the importance of the company's rich heritage to the users of this space, as does an explosion of miniature Johnson & Johnson packaging which spreads across a white wall. This commissioned artwork by Rachel Perry Welty consists of more than 600 miniature handmade replicas, from AVEENO® bottles to BAND-AID® Brand Adhesive Bandages and TYLENOL® packs, and will continue to grow over time, offering a living archive of Johnson & Johnson products.

Ribbon windows wrap around the perimeter of the space, stretching some 300 feet from one end of the studio to the other. A commitment was made not to tamper with the original windows nor block the bountiful natural light and wrap-around, daydream-inducing views. 'The windows are for everybody, not just the executives,' says Christopher March, lead architect. By pulling everything back away from the windows, a circulation corridor outlines the space, while another slices through the centre. The huge, stylistically dominating mushroom columns that structurally enable this 'curtain wall' building construction are spaced on a 20-foot grid, with low-ceilinged, glass-fronted offices respectfully sliding in-between them 'like drawers', rather than trying to 'enclose them'. The placement of these pods serves to define neighbourhoods for team placement as well as creating cosy nooks for away-from-desk activities.

Two types of desk arrangements feature in this upper-level space: booths for media planners, who require semi-privacy for frequent phone calls, and long 'Last Supper'-style tables for designers. Simply arranging design teams around one big table supports the notion of everyone working together, able to quickly share and develop ideas. Further collaboration is encouraged through ad hoc mixing of seats; neighbours might not be

FAR LEFT Tiles made from recycled wood shavings act as sound baffling and add visual interest.

LEFT A classic Charles Eames chair perches on the polished original concrete floor.

RIGHT Steel mesh curtains offer a flexible way to break up space.

working on the same project, 'which we think is good for creativity', says Hacker. 'Lotteries' are held annually to reposition people and welcome new designers into the fold. Creative Directors sit alongside the design team with a Manhattan skyline view, choosing to be 'a part of the action', reinforcing a creative mix of work style.

Rather than use off-the-shelf workstations, Johnson & Johnson chose to make bespoke arrangements, which ended up being less expensive and more appropriate for the space; a 'whiff of the industrial feel' that echoes the building is achieved through leaving plywood edges exposed and keeping things as simple as possible, 'as though someone could have fabricated them in their basement – but not quite', says Chris March. Where there are quiet spaces to escape to, glass frontages invite natural light in and, etched into the glass, the company's credo snakes its way through the spaces, its message whispering both a commitment from the executives and a guiding principle for employees. Opportunities to break out for privacy, relaxation or small-group huddles are scattered throughout, and exceed even the most collaborative office's common space to workspace ratio at an impressive 2:3; attention is paid to the quality and flexibility of these areas. End-of-booth couches and coffee tables provide places to focus (with a

ABOVE **Bulldog clip placeholders allow for regular rearrangement of team members, to encourage mixing.**

ABOVE LEFT **Semi-private booths support telephone activity and private focus for media planners and marketers.**

OPPOSITE **Designer teams share one big table, supporting the collaborative nature of their work.**

OPPOSITE The Johnson & Johnson red is used as an accent colour throughout to warm up this industrial space.

RIGHT Cornflower blue Eero Saarinen womb chairs, a pile of magazines and a view of Manhattan in one of the many away-from-desk areas.

BELOW Bamboo adds a splash of colour.

ABOVE **A retail display mock-up provides a contextual viewing environment for new concepts.**

view), welcoming colleagues from headquarters who often come to visit this satellite office and work for the day. Nooks created by the building's curves and kinks provide perfect personal think pods or lunch spots; semi-private spaces are defined by industrially elegant tin-plated steel mesh curtains.

Downstairs on the 14th floor, the NEUTROGENA® team who grew out of the 16th floor sit in new-and-improved work booths. Slightly bigger, slightly higher and surrounded by carpet, they benefit from the learning gained from occupying the original space. The rest of the floor is taken up by 'The Lab': 4,500 square feet of super-flexible space. Heavy Homasote®-lined walls on wheels provide dynamic area segmentation as well as ample pin-up space for stimuli, insights, thoughts and ideas. Comfortable sofas and chairs, coffee tables and café-style arrangements facilitate formal and informal gatherings, ideation spaces and project presentations. The space is purposefully relaxed; it is a place where people can 'open up' away from their desks. Here, the casual nature of the space turns presentations into opportunities for sharing project progress in a far more creative manner than traditional one-way PowerPoints. 'Eventually the project is captured in a formal presentation, but here, we're thinking live,' remarks Chris Hacker.

Adjacent to the main space, visually separated by mesh curtains, is a retail mock-up area. Regular supermarket shelving is left used 'just as it appears in the retail world', with lighting that emulates real stores to re-enact realistic scenarios for Johnson & Johnson and its competitors' products. Here, designers, marketers and brand teams view pack prototypes, allowing rapidly interactive form, colour and graphics development to take place. Private lab space includes a formal meeting room that doubles up as a video-conferencing facility, break-out space and project room. A digital photo-editing suite provides a valuable creative resource, alongside plans for a library and an in-house rapid prototyping suite.

Wherever possible, sustainable materials and finishes are used: linoleum desktops, low-VOC paint and pin-up surfaces made from recycled paper. The table in the reception area is made from repurposed plywood tabletops, and coffee tables are made from recycled wood scraps. In addition, tables were reused from another space. This 'saving' mentality has double-edged appeal; saving money by not spending on materials to cover up that which will one day only be discarded. The 13-foot ceiling is left bare to expose its industrial structure, and the fabulous original concrete floor has been polished to reveal its latent beauty. Sustainability is put to good creative use, with furnishings, materials and finishes often performing multiple roles at once. Tectum tiles certified by the Forest Stewardship Council (FSC) and wood shavings popularised in the 1970s as ceiling coverings are used for acoustic baffling while doubling up as a decorative accent. Applied to the wall in varying thicknesses, this sustainable finish also provides visual interest. By surrounding people with thoughtful, inherently beautiful and meaningful design the

ABOVE AND RIGHT 'The Lab': a highly flexible creative space.

A. Tables on wheels for easy manoeuvrability.

B. Homasote®-covered walls on wheels provide pin-up space and room division.

C. Durable, smooth floor for dragging furniture around.

D. Retail displays.

E. Casual seating area.

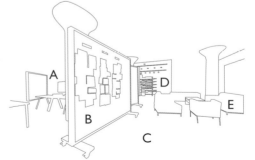

sustainability message inspires on a daily basis and is not something slapped up on the wall and forgotten. 'It's about living it, so people are thinking about it each day rather than being preached to,' says Hacker.

Johnson & Johnson's Global Strategic Design Office is a creative space that works, providing a clear focus, an aligned attitude and an inspiring space for creative minds to thrive. The proof is in the pudding; since its inception, redesigns for BAND-AID® Brand Adhesive Bandages, K-Y® Brand, JOHNSON'S® Baby Shampoo, NEUTROGENA® and AVEENO® have contributed to significant increases in sales, and design staff retention rates are at an unbelievable high. 'I'd like to think that it has something to do with the space,' says Chris March. 'I'd like to think that it has something to do with the space *and* the management!' says Chris Hacker, smiling.

THE LEGO GROUP

HEADQUARTERS, BILLUND, DENMARK

IDEA HOUSE, LØVEHUSET (THE LION HOUSE)
RECONSTRUCTED IN 1924 AFTER FIRE | RENOVATED IN 2003

PRODUCT AND MARKETING DEVELOPMENT (PMD) DESIGN STUDIO, SYSTEMVEJ
DESIGN: RUDOLF LOLK A/S, 2008

COMMUNITY, EDUCATION AND DIRECT, HAVREMARKEN
DESIGN: RUDOLF LOLK A/S, 1995

DECORATION FACTORY (THE ORIGINAL LEGO FACTORY), HØJMARKSVEJ
194,000-SQUARE-FOOT FACILITY BUILT IN 1970 | 17,000-SQUARE-FOOT EXTENSION: 1974

*Did you know ... ?
... that with a production of about 306 million tyres a year, the LEGO Group is the world's largest tyre manufacturer?*

NESTLED among the beech woods, fjords and small lakes of the flat, fertile Jutland peninsula lies the headquarters of the LEGO Group, one of Denmark's most famous exports. In 1932, Ole Kirk Christiansen, a carpenter from Billund, began making wooden toys from his workshop. In 1934, he juxtaposed the Danish words for 'play well' (*leg godt*) to create the name 'LEGO®'. The LEGO company expanded to produce plastic toys in 1947, and the brick that has won worldwide recognition was patented in 1958. Today, the LEGO brick enjoys ever-expanding appeal – from children as young as 18 months old to electronics enthusiasts and professional architects across the globe.

ABOVE The famous LEGO building brick provides a foundation for systematic play.

OPPOSITE Gigantic studs and tubes form seating booths and LEGO play-pits in a brick-inspired lobby.

LEFT The LEGO Group's headquarters is a complex of buildings that includes factory and office space.

BELOW LEFT Originally built as a family home and the LEGO Group's office in 1924, the 'Idea House' now accommodates a museum that charts the company's history and the 'Innovation Room', where future ideas are conceived.

OPPOSITE The lobby of the PMD building is a multipurpose hub – a reception, library, canteen, café and meeting space in one.

The heritage of the LEGO company, built on Danish values of hard work, humility and teamwork, remains an essential part of the LEGO Group's culture, despite its international reach. These values were recently put to the test during 'the crisis years' at the end of the 1990s, when fierce competition from interactive electronic and computer games brought the company to its knees. During this time, the company had diversified into theme parks and branded products, including clothing and multimedia games, but repeatedly reported losses of millions of dollars. In 2004, rather than selling the company, the Christiansen heirs decided to stand by it, appointing Jørgen Vig Knudstorp, a former management consultant at McKinsey, to get the company back on track. Determined to bring the company back to financial stability, Knudstorp instigated a period of intense focus, from which the company began to prosper. In 2008 the LEGO Group posted sales of 9.5 billion kroner and a 1.4 billion kroner net profit.

Today, the LEGO Group's physical spaces proudly stand as testament to the decisions taken during the recent crisis, as instead of knocking everything down and starting again, the business returned to the basic buildings and grew from there. Seven buildings track the growth of the company from the humble beginning of a carpenter's workshop through expansion of a 24,750-square-foot workshop to the complex of buildings that stand today, complete with over 970,000 square feet of mass-production capability. While there are a number of different functions across the company, a constant throughout LEGO work areas is the open space which supports the 'free flow of ideas', lots of bold colour inducing a sense of fun, and the omnipresent LEGO brick.

ABOVE **A model-maker creates in his enclosed, personalised space.**

ABOVE RIGHT **Figures in the compatible LEGO system begin life as realistic, oversized rapid-prototyping models.**

IDEA HOUSE

The original factory is now the 'Idea House', where the history of the company is displayed, preserved and re-enacted through original toys, the first plastics moulding machine, family pictures, film and audio recordings. This appreciation and celebration of the past is collocated with a space that gives birth to new ideas. In contrast to the warm and colourful heritage of the LEGO brick, the company's Innovation Room is a pure white space, with simple yet smart fixtures. Far from uninviting or stark, clues that it's safe to play include soft, flexible seating, movable panels for writing on and lava lamps that add a touch of fun. The space provides just enough guidance to indicate how it might be used without dictating. This is a place to which designers, marketers and commercial people alike come, away from their desks and their usual workspaces, to conceive new ideas. It's a place with no branding, no primary colours or miniature figurines. Etched into the glass door that separates the Innovation Room from the museum, the words of Godtfred Kirk Christiansen, who inherited the business on the death of his father Ole, seem to explain the significance of these two spaces: 'When we know the past we can better understand the present, when we understand the present, we are better equipped to meet the future.'

ABOVE AND RIGHT All white: devoid of any colour, the Innovation Room
is a blank canvas for stimulus and ideas.
A. Lightweight tables and chairs.
B. Flipcharts on wheels.
C. Low-level casual seating.
D. Semi-translucent partition screens suspended from ceiling track.

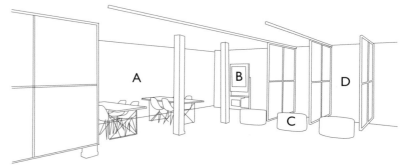

PMD – PRODUCT AND MARKETING DEVELOPMENT DESIGN STUDIO

OPPOSITE **The LEGO design and development studio, where workspaces are defined by shelving systems.**

The LEGO Group's primary concept and development work takes place here at the headquarters, where around 120 designers are based. A network of smaller 'concept labs' provide local access to major markets around the globe. In key sites such as Tokyo, Barcelona, Munich and Los Angeles, these satellite studios are the 'eyes and ears' of the LEGO firm, tracking local toy and lifestyle trends and feeding the findings back to Billund.

The PMD building houses the design studio. Refurbished in 2006 with the goal of making it a more open, creative space, the first thing that strikes you as you enter the front doors is that it's not like any other LEGO Group reception. In fact, it's not like many receptions at all. This super-collaborative space acts as a lobby, a library, a café, meeting areas and an exhibition space all in one.

The energy and mood of the place pulses through the day. The lunchtime hubbub of people connecting over meals gives way to an afternoon lull, when both structured and serendipitous meetings take place. Light, open and airy, this multi-functional space provides an air lock between the designers' studio and the rest of the LEGO business, a visual break from the colourful bricks they spend so much time with. 'Because we work so closely with the brick every day, we need something really impactful coming out of the door from the design studio – something completely different,' says Rosario Costa, Design Director. Yet the playfulness expected of the LEGO Group remains; red upholstery and lamps and bold green graphics interrupt the clean white walls, and reclaimed Baroque chairs perch high above the entryway, 'just because'. No two areas are the same, with varying table and floor heights, chairs and benches providing an open yet visually interesting space.

Behind secure doors, and off limits to all except designers and children (who are welcomed to the LEGO site for tours and co-creation events; LEGO Group employees are also encouraged to bring theirs to work), the open-plan studio bursts with activity. Team boundaries are defined by banners and brick sculptures, while designers express individuality through collected objects and imagery on display in their workspaces. Manga comics, GI JOE™ collectibles or TRANSFORMERS™ serve as inspiration for some, while the die-hard 'brick fans' can be identified by curious LEGO brick combinations that litter their desks. Although many of these half-builds seem without purpose, 'sometimes you can get inspiration from the misfit toys – the ones that didn't quite make it,' says Jamie Berard, Designer.

Project cycles can span anything from six to 18 months, and as a project gathers momentum, the team and space grows with it. In order to accommodate this flexible way of working, LEGO designers have created a shelf system that organises all of the major

NET SALES/REVENUE FROM 2004 TO 2008. SHARED VISION STRATEGY INITIATED IN 2004

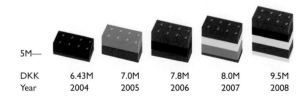

	5M—				
DKK	6.43M	7.0M	7.8M	8.0M	9.5M
Year	2004	2005	2006	2007	2008

LEGO 'elements' a designer might need. This shelving system not only makes work more effective, it's mounted on wheels, which allows teams to shift them around and form temporary boundaries.

Play is not restricted to brick-building sessions or co-creation with children, it's part of the DNA at the LEGO Group. 'Hotspots' – areas furnished with games such as table football – pop up among team spaces throughout the studio, encouraging people to relax and connect with colleagues. Inter-team competitions and tournaments are part of life here: football tournaments, a 'cow exhibition' where cow-shaped LEGO minifigures are decorated, and a blindfolded competition to tear the shape of a LEGO minifigure in paper are just some of the fun activites you'll find.

This type of playfulness relies upon a spirit of trust, something that is reinforced by the physical openness and relaxed atmosphere of the working environment. Here is a company that understands that creativity thrives when people are curious – 'when you're allowed to be playful, when you're allowed to harness your imagination by asking "what if something was completely different?" or asking stupid questions,' as Cecilia Weckstrom, Experience and Innovation Director explains. This curiosity is fuelled by an appreciation and appetite for learning, and one of the many ways that learning happens here is when people meet, randomly exchanging ideas or finding inspiration in something they see on a neighbour's desk or overhear in a corridor. These connections are the essential thing that builds friendships – and 'friendships are the thing that allows you come to terms with the vulnerability that sometimes accompanies hair-brained ideas,' remarks Weckstrom. The environment at the LEGO Group reflects that way of thinking through making the spaces as open and light as possible, encouraging serendipitous encounters wherever possible and filling the space with toys.

LEFT Freshly manufactured LEGO pieces stacked in colour-coded crates according to element type.

OPPOSITE The Billund factory accounts for around 70% of all LEGO bricks manufactured. About 19 billion are made every year here, equivalent to two million elements an hour, or 36,000 a minute.

OPPOSITE BELOW A wide corridor filled with fun activities for mid-meeting energy boosts.

PRODUCTION

Around 70 per cent of LEGO components are still produced out of the Billund factory: the moulding, assembly and decoration machines produce approximately 19 billion per year, or about 600 pieces per second. Yet the playfulness of the brand is seen even in this manufacturing space; sculpted LEGO murals and colourful canvas paintings decorate walls, and the enormous warehouse shelving system is stacked with colourful boxes retrieved by an automated picker.

The 'Concept Factory', located off the main mass-production floor, is where engineers and scientists experiment with new materials and manufacturing techniques. A mini factory-within-a-factory, it also supports pilot runs of new ideas and special-edition short runs, making it a flexible creative tool in addition to the mass-production capability.

COMMUNITY, EDUCATION AND DIRECT (CED)

Despite the greater focus on its core product, the LEGO Group has retained small parts of its diversification strategy, specifically those endeavours that have strong roots in the essence of the brand. 'Community' builds on the deep relationship that fans have with LEGO products, 'Education' addresses the learning aspect of the brand, and 'Direct' looks at alternative ways of engaging and accessing consumers. Created to engage in a one-to-one dialogue with LEGO brick users, the CED division is located in one of the former factories – a lofty saw-toothed ceiling with exposed wooden beams and raw industrial ducts, and now home to a lobby that welcomes visitors into oversized LEGO brick-inspired seating and pits full of bricks.

Supporting disciplines from product development to community relations and education, the workspaces comprise basic desking wrapped in a warm wood, big open spaces and of course lots and lots of LEGO components. Bowls filled with LEGO bricks adorn meeting room tables, play areas are scattered throughout the workspaces, and with lots of products, toys and games around, it's difficult not to want to play. Purposely wide corridor areas are more like playgrounds where employees on electric scooters weave between basketball hoops and a swing, and an oversized chair reminds the LEGO Group staff what it feels like to be a child. 'It's important to play and have fun to keep the inner child alive – keep reminding ourselves what it's like to be a child – it's part of our job and our mentality,' says Rosario Costa.

Here, you'll often see children running around in corridors and playing in nooks and crannies. 'When spaces are child-friendly, it takes away a lot of the hierarchy and the stuffiness that many corporate environments have where they almost indirectly put you on the defensive, make you wonder whether you look grown up enough, know what you're talking about,' remarks Cecilia Weckstrom, which ultimately makes people 'play it safe more often rather than putting yourself out there,' which in turn stifles creativity.

The LEGO Group has looked back at its history, reconnected with its core and found new ways of applying creativity to business. By developing a better understanding of what they do and what's important to their fans, they've built a culture that aspires to be 'systematically creative' across the board with the effect that creativity is a part of daily life. The environments provide clues for creative behaviour, but hold back from prescribing any particular way of being, and this in turn provides a framework for creativity that is far more than just a blank canvas.

The LEGO Group's playfulness is inherent both in its products and in its people, and by adding playful touches throughout its spaces, it encourages a relaxed sense of creativity. While some companies throw big, wacky and 'out there' objects into their environments in an effort to inspire, at the LEGO Group, a humble, practical approach is taken to the spaces, and the lessons they've learnt over their colourful history serve them well to build great things in the future. After all, as Paal Smith-Meyer, Director New Business, says: 'Everything big starts small.'

NIKE, INC.

NIKE WORLD HEADQUARTERS, BEAVERTON, OREGON, USA
DESIGN: IN-HOUSE TEAMS SINCE 1990

Did you know ...?
... that the turf on the Bo Jackson Field at WHQ is made from 'Nike Grind', a rubber compound made from around 40,000 recycled shoes as part of Nike's Reuse-A-Shoe Program?

A S you enter Nike World Headquarters, the pristine lawns, great glass buildings, marble fountains and bronze statues convey the grandeur and professionalism one would expect from a brand with Nike's reputation and track record. Yet chaos has been welcomed into this perfect picture, with a unique subculture that permeates throughout the organisation. Nike is the world's leading supplier of athletic shoes, apparel and sports equipment with annual revenue in excess of US$19 billion in 2009, employing over 30,000 people across six continents. But it's more than that. With its origins in sport and entrepreneurship, Nike's growth has been achieved through balancing a sharp competitive streak with a genuinely inclusive nature.

ABOVE Nike is the world's largest and most recognised athletic footwear and apparel brand.

OPPOSITE A communal area in the Michael Jordan building which is imbued with the spirit of the basketball legend through memorabilia and inspiring quotes.

ABOVE **One Bowerman Drive. Arrival at WHQ is a grand gesture to co-founder Bill Bowerman.**

BELOW LEFT AND RIGHT **World-class facilities cater for a diverse range of sporting activities, for everyone from armchair followers to keep-fit enthusiasts to professional athletes.**

The precursor to Nike, Blue Ribbon Sports, was founded in 1964 by University of Oregon track and field coach Bill Bowerman and Phil Knight, who ran under Bowerman from 1955 to 1959. Bowerman was known for his unique coaching methods, often tinkering with existing training shoes to suit his runners; and Knight, after graduating from Stanford University, exercised his entrepreneurial muscles through importing Japanese running shoes to future rival adidas. Bowerman and Knight joined forces to distribute and later to design and make their own running shoes, employing co-runner Jeff Johnson in 1965, founding Nike, Inc. in 1972 and signing their first sponsored athlete in 1978.

Situated on the outskirts of Portland, Oregon, Nike's World Headquarters (WHQ) is set on 192 acres of lush green land that includes 17 buildings of just over 2 million square feet, two Olympic-standard sports centres, a 6-acre lake and natural wetlands. A haven for around 5,000 sports and fitness fans (aka employees), the home of this epic brand is not only the closest thing to the best sports university one could attend, but it also acts as a storybook telling tales of great winners in sport and business that helps keep the 'Just Do It' spirit alive.

RIGHT Bronze statues dotted throughout the grounds pay tribute to sport. The Jeff Johnson running trail loops 1.9 miles around the campus.

TRIBUTE TO LEGENDS

In the same way that athletes face challenges as they strive towards their goals, over the years Nike as a business has had to endure intense competition, overcome public hurdles and deal with tough criticism. Throughout, the environment has remained a constant source of encouragement, inspiration and support for employees. The WHQ campus is a physical embodiment of the Nike brand – resonating with examples of the athletic spirit and inspired by the strength, skill, passion and personality of athletes. Just as the brand is built on products that have a real performance history, the Nike work environment is built on authentic stories baked into the environment which manifest themselves in a multitude of ways, from the life-size bronze statues of sporting heroes to the Japanese Gardens whose footbridge represents the link with Nissho Iwai, the company that funded Nike as a fledgling business.

The buildings on campus are named after legendary athletes and are awash with memorabilia, inspiring quotes and photographs depicting defining moments. Even the running trails that loop around the campus are named after Nike's first full-time employee, Jeff Johnson, who is credited with coming up with the Nike name. These stories, continually reflected in the environment, remind employees that through hard work, dedication and a spirit to win, great things can happen.

OPPOSITE The bridge in the Nissho Iwai Japanese Gardens symbolises the link between Nike and the company that provided early financial backing.

BELOW Covered walkways connecting the main building on Nike's campus are lined with tributes to sporting heroes.

A PLACE TO LEARN AND GROW

Knight and Bowerman wanted to create an environment where people can learn, grow and continually strive to be better, and so Nike's college-style campus was deliberately designed to provide an informal, open community feel. There are no suits, rather people of all ages, lots of smiley faces – saying 'hello' to each other as they walk by, stopping to talk on the grass, in the courtyard or on covered walkways. Old-timers coach bright, fresh new talent and they learn from one another, the campus-style facilities and atmosphere encouraging this behaviour.

On-site facilities run the full gamut of sports and fitness activities from women's yoga to golf to youth skateboarding, extending beyond sport and into the lifestyles that surround employees, including two paternity centres for over 400 children and an organic farmers' market. This great environment provides a very comfortable, healthy and convenient way of life. Located in the 'green state' of Oregon, near the confluence of two rivers and with scores of national parks in the surrounding landscapes, outdoor activity is a feature of daily life, and it is difficult not to lead a healthy lifestyle. Jessica Giannini, Head of Design Recruitment, remarks on its effect on employees: 'There's an encouragement of enjoying the space that you work in and taking advantage of the campus, it's the perfect enticer.'

Yet, surprisingly, not all Nike employees are super-fit! While sport performance is at the heart of their brand, its diversity and mass appeal means that a friendly buzz of inclusiveness is reflected in the people who work at Nike and the way the spaces are approached. You don't have to be a top athlete to work here, because, in the words of the late Bill Bowerman, 'if you have a body, you are an athlete'.

CONSUMER FOCUS

In 2004/5, after a stumble in the late 1990s, Nike reorganised its functional, product-led teams (footwear, apparel, equipment, etc) into six categories (Running, Basketball, Football (soccer), Athletic Training, Women and Nike Sportswear), a strategic shift that assembled cross-functional teams around a more consumer-led approach. Nike had already established an unbeatable strategy of combining high-tech products with endorsements from elite athletes, but this new approach moved them closer to their core consumer. Since then, the physical spaces have seen changes that better reflect this way of working. Physically bringing these multi-disciplined teams together in centres of excellence and immersing them in a specific category has dramatically increased the speed with which teams communicate as well as the ease of idea sharing. Jeff Cha, Consumer Cultures Director, observes that 'it makes what's been happening anyway happen more. Co-location physically has made the way we work so much more powerful.' The resulting opportunities are endless. Released from the limitations of functional silos (when a designer would conceive a shoe in relative isolation), teams can get to know everything about the world of a 24-year-old female gym-goer, for example, understand her needs and subsequently create a holistic solution of footwear, apparel and supporting accessories.

ABOVE **A typical Nike design workspace.**

ABOVE TOP **Army surplus snow camouflage net makes an informal space partition.**

OPPOSITE **The office of Sandy Bodecker, Vice President of Global Design. It is filled with inspiration and memorabilia surrounding two of his many passions: soccer and skateboarding.**

LEFT AND BELOW Casual ideation pods are primed, ready for use:

A. Filing cabinets form focused yet open ideation pods with pin-up space.

B. Natural light and wonderful views promote the right creative state.

C. Storage files on wheels and bins filled with supplies – everything you need for an ideas session.

D. Comfortable seating and low tables encourage relaxed ideas sharing.

E. Whiteboard tabletops for quick capture.

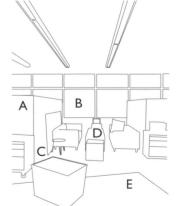

BRINGING THE OUTSIDE IN

Intense immersion in any subject brings the concomitant risk that one can lose sight of one's surroundings. Combined with their fantastic facilities, it would be easy for Nike people to be caught in a bubble, locked in a comfortable world of sport as they know it. One of the ways that Nike avoids such myopia, alongside external design trips and market-related consumer research, is through the Consumer Cultures space, a place where anyone at Nike can come to be inspired. The team that lives here acts as an internal consultancy, filling the space with easy-to-access information about the world outside, and whose mission is to catalyse and enable the culture of insights and innovation at Nike. Here, they hold a dialogue of 'informed intuition' through deep-dive ethnographic research, which takes a journalistic approach to the discovery and sharing of consumer knowledge.

The space was formerly a library, and when the Consumer Cultures team moved in they slimmed books down from 12,000 to around 5,000 rare and inspiring titles and knocked down walls to create a more dynamic resource. A protected space, people 'cross a line' when they enter, leaving their 'other knowledge at the door and letting this stuff soak in', says Jeff Cha. Blackboard-painted walls are filled with 'did you know?' factoids that change on a regular basis, communicating that this is a place of curiosity. A welcoming concierge desk sweeps visitors in, past the open book collection and vast array of global magazine publications, to the 'Fresh Today' area, where the most current things happening in the marketplace are posted. Adjacent to this is a trend-tracking wall, littered with Post-its® of thoughts. Sofas, beanbags and tables with writable surfaces break up this open-plan area into small, functional ideas spaces. Partitions are created with freestanding filing cabinets, and stackable foam blocks act as chairs as well as create temporary walls. Ideation boxes on wheels are filled with all the materials one might need for an informal ideas session.

No longer simply a library or information resource, this is a place where people can go to find out about consumers and their lives. Jeff Cha explains the importance of providing the opportunity to turn information into something more tangible when he says: 'An insight or foresight without application is just an interesting observation or purpose. Here people have a functional space where they can take the resources and insights and then ideate on the spot with their team.' The Consumer Cultures resource is a functional place of discovery, where anyone at Nike can tap into the 'heartbeat of culture', be inspired and turn that inspiration into ideas.

ABOVE At the Consumer Cultures Center, global trends and consumer insights are gathered and presented in an easy-to-digest format on a curved wall.

BELOW An open resource available to all Nike employees, a library of around 5,000 books and up-to-date periodicals from around the world provides inspiration.

IN IT TO WIN IT

To succeed in sport is to win – and so it is with innovation at Nike. As the most innovative business in their field, Nike has always invested heavily in advanced research and development, never afraid to try things out for the first time. In order to maintain an advantage over the competition, the Innovation Kitchen exists to explore and develop 'beyond next generation' footwear and equipment ideas that are two to 20 years out, compared with Nike's typical design cycle of 24 months. This exclusive creativity zone is home to a small group of 'maverick' designers who, instead of spending their budget on space or external consultancies, found a forgotten, unused space that was formerly occupied by resident chefs.

Protected from the commercial pressure that typically exists in the main Nike business, the 'Kitchen' has its own design process separate from the in-line design process, preserving its free attitude and sense of exploration. Responsible for much of the Nike product innovation debuted at the Beijing Olympics, Nike's Innovation Kitchen has generated hundreds of patents. Commercial successes include the Nike Flywire technology, used in a track shoe which weighs less than an ounce that uses support thread, an innovation based on the same principle as the steel cables in a suspension bridge, to replace the running shoe's typically heavy structural materials. The success of the Innovation Kitchen has had an effect on more than just the bottom line. It is seen as an essential cog of Nike's Innovation machine and a reflection of Nike's wider culture, with its origins tracing back to Bill Bowerman's own garage. What started out as an experiment at WHQ six years ago, the latest incarnation of the Innovation Kitchen has grown from a small team of 12 people to a group of around 75, with expanded premises.

Importantly, it was the ownership of this space as well as its relative lack of glitz that fostered the spirit essential for the Innovation team. In contrast to the more conventional office spaces on campus, the Kitchen's open and rough industrial spaces elicit social interaction and curiosity and a way of working that was unfamiliar to some. Part of the leadership challenge has been in bringing people who are more familiar with individual working spaces into a very open, dynamic and collaborative environment. Thus, maintaining the right balance of openness and privacy is important and has been achieved through the creation of 'zones and homes'. While visually open, the Innovation Kitchen has themed neighbourhoods based on specific expertise, and within those zones, more intimate groupings of eight to 12 people reside. The only rule in the Kitchen is that there are strictly no cubes. Mark Smith, Creative Director for Brand Jordan, exclaims: '"Kill the box" is a term we use lovingly. Because we're all about thinking outside of it.'

A key ingredient that has contributed to the Innovation Kitchen's success is a diversity of experience and backgrounds. The team comprises industrial, fashion, footwear and graphic designers, ethnographers and artists, whose disparate views on the world come together to create a level of chaos. 'Creatives are emotionally driven. Their response to the chaos is to form unity in answering those questions,' explains Mark Smith. The resulting answers are new-to-the-world, surprising ideas.

PUSHING TO THE LIMIT

The Nike Research Lab is a place where scientists, engineers, designers and athletes come together to go that extra mile. Once product concepts are developed, they are tested to the limits to make sure that not only are they out there first, but they're the best they can possibly be. Here, people from all walks of life with all sorts of skills converge to make, test and develop products. Biologists, plastics engineers, mechanical engineers, cobblers and 'stitchers' combine to enable a quick product creation process. An idea can come in from the Innovation Kitchen in the morning and by the end of the day it will have been built and tested on an athlete, with raw data outputs for review and refinement. Super-high-speed photography captures landing, takeoff and impact information. Biometric, pressure and visual deformation information feeds the process of 'measure, quantify and improve'. It's a highly dynamic, highly experimental, hands-dirty environment. 'There's a lot of guerrilla science that goes on here. We can take an idea and gut instinct and with the tools we have here, we can come up with some pretty quick evaluations,' says Mark Smith. If a process for making and testing a new product doesn't exist, they create it: for the Flywire shoe, they had to break a machine to create a new one that would do what they wanted it to do.

In a recent move to seamlessly blend the brains and talent of the Kitchen with the Sports Research Lab, the 'functional symbolism' of tearing down the walls – creating open areas with shared spaces – is one that will fuel the extreme concept development process further. Physically linking the spaces is a curved wall that bridges the three disciplines, and right down the centre in what used to be a hallway is a running track, where new shoes and products can be tested quickly. This is where science meets art, a marriage of the creative 'what if' with the tangible as well as the persistence of trial and testing. It is the place where ideas become reality.

As Nike constantly strives to win and continues to challenge itself, there are devices built into the campus that cause Nike people to pause, lift their spirits and help them to sustain their performance. A walk along a tree-lined path in the Japanese Gardens, sitting on a bench by the lake, or enjoying a drink in the Sports Bar – Nike's WHQ provides the perfect environment for getting the most from its people. They've found the perfect recipe for combining an inclusive environment with a competitive spirit. But, just when things were beginning to feel a little too perfect, they've shaken it up, injected a little chaos and are making this comfortable bubble just a little uncomfortable in order to keep the competitive spirit alive.

ABOVE Product trials in the Nike Sports Research Lab make use of high-speed photography, environment chambers, pressure-sensing equipment and lots of 'guerrilla science'.

OPPOSITE Lake Nike: a 6-acre man-made tranquil expanse of water encircled by quiet, tree-lined paths.

OAKLEY

OAKLEY, INC., THE BUNKER, FOOTHILL RANCH, CALIFORNIA, USA
ARCHITECT AND DESIGN: COLIN BADEN, 1997

Did you know...? ... that Oakley was named after the founder Jim Jannard's dog?

PERCHED on top of a decapitated hill in southern California, the headquarters of sunglasses manufacturer Oakley could be taken for a post-apocalyptic fortress from an alien planet. It is aptly described on Oakley's website as 'a place of reinforced blast walls and the padded cells of mad science'. This anachronistic design bunker is where all of Oakley's products and technologies are invented, developed, tested and perfected and manufactured. Even the packaging and advertising is handled in-house. Provocative, industrial and iconic, Oakley's headquarters conveys the brand's bold personality and virtues to all who dare to enter.

ABOVE The Oakley Jawbone sunglasses feature switchlock technology that allows sports professionals to change lenses quickly with minimal handling and optimal convenience.

OPPOSITE The unique facade of Oakley, Inc.'s headquarters in Southern California makes a provocative statement to onlookers: 'Come in if you dare!'

ABOVE New arrivals are 'welcomed' by a torpedo.

ABOVE RIGHT They have a tank … a tank!

OPPOSITE 'The Bunker': 3-foot-deep windows and huge buttresses imply impregnability.

In 1975, self-professed 'mad scientist' Jim Jannard saw an opportunity to make a better handgrip for motocross bikes. With an initial investment of $300 he invented Unobtainium®, a rubber that increases its grip with sweat (and so named because the composition was difficult to achieve), and sold his 'Oakley Grips' out of the back of his car at motocross events. He gave some of the sport's top professional riders free grips, believing their endorsement of the product to be the best form of marketing. The grips looked and performed like nothing else and soon a buzz developed among elite riders. Although the grips were successful, Jannard had a problem: the riders' hands were covering the logo he sought to publicise! So Jannard shifted his focus to inventing an innovative goggle with superior visibility. The 'O-Frame' drew inspiration from the perfect form of a cylinder and its unusual style caught the attention of pro riders. Again, the product was championed, this time with the 'Oakley' logo boldly featured on the head strap; television coverage of motocross events and post-race interviews thus provided free advertising.

Oakley's genesis is rooted in sound principles that are alive and kicking in the business today: design products that provide superior performance for elite athletes and challenge contemporary technical and aesthetic 'norms'; design them so they stand apart from the mainstream; and let select people talk about them. Even the executive team are nonconformist. The CEO of the company, Colin Baden, was originally an architect whom Jannard engaged to design the perfect home, chosen because he summarised his interpretation of Jannard's vision in a sketch of a pyramid and a freight train. That home has never been built but instead the essence of those ideas has been channelled into the headquarters. After finishing the project, Baden became the Head of Design at Oakley and has led the team to create iconic products such as Oakley Jawbone and Gascan. It's no wonder that the headquarters for Oakley is dramatic, unconventional and a place where crazy inventions come with the territory.

ABOVE Bolts the size of your head.

PROTECTION

As you sweep round 'Icon' drive, you're hit by an ominous sight: a towering grey slab of a fortress with enormous spikes jutting out and buttresses so deep they look as though they could withstand a nuclear holocaust. And then there's the torpedo pointing right between your eyes. This bold, looming monster of a building reflects Oakley's assertive, nonconformist attitude and screams 'don't mess with us!'. Its main function is to provide protection for ideas, and with blast-proof walls, spikes and weaponry, it demonstrates a commitment to protecting Oakley's position at the cutting edge of sports equipment.

Everything at Oakley is about pushing the envelope, being bold, cranking up the volume. A provocative attitude radiates throughout the building: 3-foot-deep windows cast heavy shadows in the intense glare of the sun, buttresses amplify the depth of the walls while over-scale features heighten the drama. Step through heavy unmarked doors of an imposing facade modelled on the Indian headdress found on an old 25-cent piece, and into the mother of all lobbies. A vaulted space, it is dominated by an enormous, functioning extractor fan, and includes B-52 bomber ejector seats, structural bolts the size of your head and explosion-proof strip lighting.

Despite this defensive exterior, there is a remarkably generous atmosphere inside. Friendly faces, casual dress, open doors, with anyone from the janitor to the CEO wearing shorts and flip-flops. The rigid uniformity of the externally facing physical environment affords flexibility, freedom and individuality on an inside where people feel free to experiment, take risks, jump off the edge, fall down once in a while, get back up and try it all over again. This place attracts irreverent people, who have 'gotta be somewhat tough,' says Baden: 'If you can get past the lobby and feel inspired not intimidated, then you'll fit just fine.' In fact you'll thrive. The message that it's OK to fail in the pursuit of success is displayed in the fallen products that proudly tell tales of bravery and innovation.

Beyond the lobby, where battle-scarred snowboards and other team Oakley trophies are propped up among the buttresses, a walkthrough of the company's history is archived chronologically behind glass by the products that built Oakley's success and personality. Iconic artefacts sit side-by-side with products that the company is famous for. Some bold and outrageous 'failures' are also displayed, including a hingeless sunglasses frame that curves over the top of the head and a sculpted shoe made from bulletproof vest fibres. While neither was financially successful, they represent an important aspect of Oakley's philosophy and underlying culture. Creating an atmosphere where failing is celebrated encourages a spirit of boldness and bravery, which in turn pushes people to try things that have never been tried before. Oakley's design intent is to 'reinvent what was possible by ignoring what the world thinks something should be. Or could be,' says Baden.

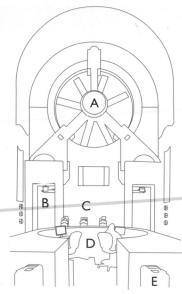

LEFT AND ABOVE The cavernous lobby creates a dramatic backdrop.

A. Huge ventilation fans.

B. Blast-proof light fixtures.

C. Ejector seats from B-52 bombers found in an old Air Force 'graveyard'.

D. The reception desk evokes a sci-fi command station.

E. Props include jerry cans.

CONTROL (FREAKS)

Oakley can afford to take risks. By controlling virtually everything through the process, from concept to packaging and marketing, risk is mitigated. In fact, with manufacturing, engineering, frame moulding, lens coating, assembling and testing all managed under one roof, the unknowns that some might view as risks look more like opportunities to explore or experiment here. 'Everything you see, feel, taste about the brand happens out of this facility,' confirms Scott Bowers, Senior Vice President, Global Marketing and former Oakley sponsored athlete.

High-tech labs, extreme experimentation, meticulous manufacturing – Oakley's obsessive compulsion to solve 'impossible' challenges is made possible by its capability to control the details: owning and creating machines, testing equipment, and inventing new materials, coatings and products. Equipped with the latest 3D scanning, printing and coating machines, Oakley's designers and engineers test and tweak, controlling everything: 'When you control all the data, what comes out is exactly, exactly what we developed,' says Baden. With these facilities and the capability to control the entire creation process, there is no dilution of the idea and problems can be solved along the way with designers, engineers and technicians all working together to achieve the vision as first conceived.

Guarded by a military diorama, Oakley's design lab is a secure area where designers develop new product ideas. A set of rules guide, but don't dictate their design, encouraging designers to act as hunter-gatherers for inspiration, to redefine what's physically possible and to seek solutions that elevate physics to the level of art. Oakley's design, development and engineering teams step up to 'impossible' challenges, reinventing from scratch and delivering the unexpected. Epic production and technical challenges are taken head-on, such as 'Thump', performance eyewear with built-in MP3 – a project that went from scratch to shelf in three months, despite involving over 150 parts and 28 vendors. The design bunker is a busy maze of booths and desks, all in that gunmetal grey, where clusters of designers draw, model and discuss ideas.

In test labs, products are challenged to withstand high-speed steel shot and falling metal spikes in home-developed 'product torture chambers'. This in-house capability not only allows Oakley to develop high-quality products, but to experiment and invent on the fly – they have an idea, mock it up, test it, then manufacture it. Oakley doesn't limit its concepts to existing technical capabilities: as Jim Jannard explains, 'we don't design ideas to fit machines, we make machines to fit ideas.' Surprisingly, having intense control over the environment and the things they create provides Oakley with an amazing

SALES FIGURES SINCE THE MOVE TO THE CURRENT HEADQUARTERS.

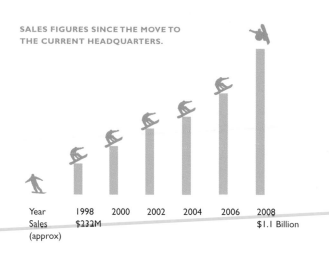

Year	1998	2000	2002	2004	2006	2008
Sales (approx)	$232M					$1.1 Billion

BELOW LEFT Out back, a fire pit becomes the focal point for parties at Oakley.

BELOW Manufacturing and distribution is handled on-site, ensuring complete quality control.

BELOW LEFT High-precision testing facilities are often invented to push the limits of technical excellence.

BELOW MIDDLE Oakley pushes ideas to breaking point behind secure doors.

BELOW RIGHT A 400-seat amphitheatre accommodates whole-company meetings, celebrations and events.

OPPOSITE B-52 bomber ejector seats for visitors who are brave enough.

platform for bold experimentation, or what could be described as flexibility within a structure or spontaneity within a plan.

From the skull and crossbones branded on the CEO's door to a framed news article depicting the rebellious nature of the company's marketing campaigns, Oakley's spaces reflect the fun with which they like to provoke. Oakley does not design for the masses. Their products are made with elite iconic athletes in mind. You'll not find focus groups here. 'We speak to the front row; they're the ones who get our jokes,' says Baden. Oakley would rather offend the majority and excite the few who share the same level of passion for living on the edge. There are secrets within secrets deep inside the catacombs of the bunker that reinforce the exclusive nature of the brand. With places to discover and stories that unfold as you explore, this place is not for everyone. But even if you're not one of the die-hard Oakley brand followers that work there, it's difficult not to wonder what mad inventions are being conceived next.

Inspired by the 'beautiful' forms of weaponry and the machined ellipse of the Oakley 'O', and with steampunk references to pyramids and freight trains, the bunker is truly unique. A highly efficient problem-solving machine wrapped in a provocative visual statement, this iconic space – like Oakley's products – is, to some, 'physics elevated to an art form'.

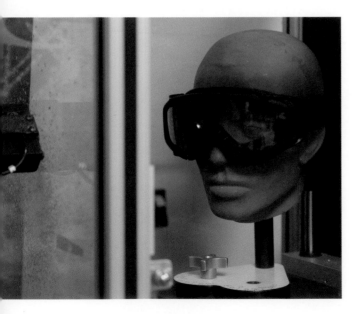

PHILIPS

PHILIPS DESIGN

PHILIPS DESIGN HEADQUARTERS, DE WITTE DAME (THE WHITE LADY), EINDHOVEN, THE NETHERLANDS
BUILT AT THE END OF THE 1920s FOR PHILIPS | ORIGINAL ARCHITECT: DIRK ROZENBURG
DESIGN: BERT DIRRIX, EARLY 1990s

PHILIPS DESIGN HONG KONG, PHILIPS ELECTRONICS BUILDING, HONG KONG SCIENCE PARK, HONG KONG
SCIENCE PARK ARCHITECT: SIMON KWAN & ASSOCIATES LTD
DESIGN: PDM INTERNATIONAL, WITH IN-HOUSE TEAM VINCENT VAUCELLE AND EDWARD TONINO

ROYAL PHILIPS ELECTRONICS was founded in 1891; its first products were light bulbs and other electro-technical equipment. Philips boomed with the widespread adoption of electricity at the end of the 19th century and today it is one of the largest electronics companies in the world with approximately 116,000 employees globally. Philips Design HQ was built in 1928 on the site of a former Philips lighting factory, when the decision was taken to move to consumer electronics. At a time when design was little more than an afterthought, the agency was primarily created to provide advertising to the mass market. Since then, Philips Design has become a rudder for the wider company, whose aim is to become a truly design-led organisation, placing real emphasis on creating things that consumers want to use, rather than simply what looks cool.

ABOVE The Philips Wake-up Light simulates sunrise for a gentle start to the day.

OPPOSITE The reception at Philips Design's Hong Kong office. A splash of orange makes a simple accent throughout the studio.

Creative but not zany, simple but not dull, sensible but not boring. Philips Design is the creative engine of Royal Philips Electronics and design consultancy to a number of external Fortune 500 companies. From baby monitors to MRI scanners, toothbrushes to advanced urban lighting systems, Philips Design focuses on simplifying human experiences through insightful and carefully considered consumer products, healthcare and lighting solution – and has received countless awards for design innovation.

A visit to any of their studios across the world reveals beautifully functional working environments that balance exploration and chaos with relevance and meaning. These quietly confident spaces reflect Philips Design's brand values and culture, and a commitment to providing down-to-earth solutions, driven by a genuine desire to improve people's quality of life. Headquartered in Eindhoven, The Netherlands, Philips Design became an independent unit within the Philips Group in 1998. Its eight studios across the world employ a diverse mix of around 500 professionals from the more traditional functions of industrial and product design to body architecture, fashion design, trend research and futurology.

Philips Design's mission is to bring 'sense and simplicity' to a world where complexity increasingly touches our daily lives through design, and it is this vision that has driven the company's collective psyche as well as the brand's value, with revenues from new products rising from 25 per cent in 2003 to 49 per cent in 2005. The 'sense and simplicity' philosophy translates clearly into the environments within which these designers and researchers work, and is as evident in the Headquarters renovated 10 years ago as it is in a recent renovation in the studio space in Hong Kong.

In Eindhoven, de Witte Dame (The White Lady) is one of the city's most striking buildings and is steeped with heritage. But this old building is home to a vibrant collection of young, fresh talent; Philips Design shares it with the Central Library and the Design Academy. Maintaining a sense of the industrial nature of the building, a minimalist architectural approach was chosen, its materials, environmental systems and flexible layout ensuring that the space still works after a decade. The carpet, chosen for its hard-wearing properties and asphalt look, was installed during the original refurbishment, yet looks brand new. In high-traffic areas, such as the stairways and lifts, tough yet beautiful marine wood warms the industrial materials of concrete and steel. Investment in long-lasting, functional elements and furniture makes for a space that is timeless and unassuming, not overwhelmingly 'designed' or stimulating in a particular way, and that does not go out of fashion. This all contributes to spaces that stand the test of time, and that are low-cost and respectful of the environment in that frequent, costly refurbishments are not necessary.

TOP Philips Design Hong Kong sits on a Science Park that overlooks Tolo Harbour.

ABOVE Philips Design Headquarters in Eindhoven is a former light bulb factory.

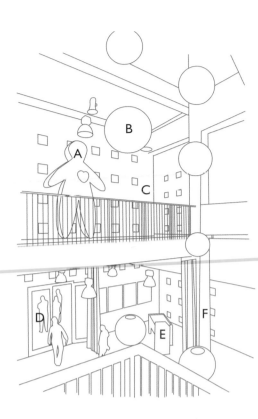

RIGHT AND ABOVE A core cut through the middle of the Eindhoven building creates a connecting atrium.

A. A reminder that people are at the heart of everything the Philips Design team create.

B. A simple yet striking lighting solution draws attention to the vast stairway shaft.

C. A glass feature lets light in and complies with fire regulations.

D. Open to all – a place for weekly colloquia, formal gatherings and parties.

E. Table football sits on the ground floor, adjacent to a 'serious' coffee machine for impromptu challenges.

F. Curtains create temporary private spaces for confidential meetings and presentations.

ABOVE An idea pod in the Hong Kong office provides an inclusive yet focused space for creative sessions.

HONG KONG

Philips Design Hong Kong is situated in the same building as the parent company, Philips Electronics, on the Hong Kong Science Park overlooking the Tolo Harbour in the north-east New Territories of Hong Kong. Built in 2001, the sleek and contemporary steel, concrete and glass construction boasts the modern style one would expect from a business park, but is imbued with a compelling twist. The roof of the structure evokes one of a Chinese Temple with its upwardly curving overhang and grand columned facade.

The Hong Kong studio is home to around 80 people led by Edward Tonino, Senior Branch Director, who set out in 2006 to create a space that would be home to a growing team of new talent, keeping them engaged and inspired. One of the challenges he faced was that of creating a space that was still part of the organisation yet would retain its own identity. The studio needed to be inspiring and engaging for designers, encouraging creative behaviour and supporting design activity. Additionally, an expanding team would mean growing out of the space and to a new location at some point in the future, so an important factor was to minimise infrastructural changes and enable them to pick up and move if necessary.

The solution for Tonino's team lay in an open-plan studio which, arranged in a U-shape that skirts the edges of the super-glazed building, allows natural light in and views out onto the harbour and courtyard below. Around 70 designers sit in small groups of four to six that share bench-style desks. Sliding storage cabinets that double up as graphic presentation space and white, back-painted partition walls that also act as writing surfaces are some of the simple yet effective ideas you'll find here. A pantry with bar seating, adjacent to a resource library, adds to the relaxed yet professional nature of the studio. Here, information is exchanged casually over coffee. While retaining some of the familiar trappings of corporate office buildings (tiled carpet floors and false ceilings), this open configuration, with its coffee bar and comfortable casual seating, works contrary to many Chinese offices. Bright orange pods, created in simple 7-foot-high walls with radiused corners, are dropped into the space, providing private yet inclusive areas for idea generation, small team huddles or quiet time.

There is a certain style that comes with keeping things simple, and that simplicity can be found in these spaces: nowhere will you see gimmicks or quirks – everything is fit for purpose and well considered. Philips spaces are not 'fantastic' or 'extrovert', they employ raw, modest, industrial materials, with thoughtful touches of colour and vibrancy to make them feel human. 'We don't need lots of extra colour since the chaos of the creative process takes over,' says Tonino. An environment that takes these qualities into consideration is one that is not over-complicated, functions appropriately and makes people feel comfortable.

ABOVE AND OPPOSITE The Hong Kong office layout supports the flexibility and functionality required by designers, while modular pods allow for a change of location should the company need to move.

LEFT The fully stocked pantry that backs onto a magazine resource is a place where information is shared casually.

ABOVE Formal meeting rooms, offices and project rooms maintain a balance of privacy and inclusiveness with textured glass.

ABOVE RIGHT Dotted throughout the spacious studio are numerous places that facilitate quick ideas exchanges.

VALUE OF THE PHILIPS BRAND

| 4.3 | 5.9 | 6.7 | 7.7 | 8.3 | $US Billion |
| 2004 | 2005 | 2006 | 2007 | 2008 | Year |

FLUIDITY

Philips Design supports its creative endeavours through nurturing and mixing an exciting breadth of skills, experience and passion. People-focused and multidisciplinary, this 'Renaissance organisation' requires its spaces to accommodate a broad range of working styles, personalities and activities. Critical to its success is the exchange of experience, information and ideas. The central staircase in the Eindhoven building allows for fluid movement through the space, connecting sightlines across all floors. Casual meeting spaces, formal ideas booths, mug-shots of employees and the projects they've worked on posted on pillars and in coffee areas, are all simple solutions that combine to create a powerfully collaborative effect.

Just as Philips Design teams are composed of people with varying specialisations, the organisation as a whole benefits from location-specific strengths. Work is distributed depending on each studio's 'centre of gravity'. For example Eindhoven is centre for Design, Research and Innovation, whereas Amsterdam is centre for Communication Design. There is a constant flow of people and knowledge through these spaces, requiring both structured and casual transfer of knowledge. The Philips Design Cultural Program is integral to the way that Philips Design shares design knowledge throughout its creative community. This training programme expands and aligns the creative capabilities of designers by deploying gained knowledge into the entire organisation with tools they can later utilise to apply this knowledge within the design process. More casual cross-pollination exists in the form of people meeting at events, travelling from studio to studio and taking with them information they've gathered along the way. This 'fluidity', where people act as the means of information transfer, requires the physical environment to act as a conduit for ideas; the spaces must be able to adapt to the people moving through them, through evolving technologies and accommodating different work styles and projects.

As much of the work is project based, Philips spaces typically provide many 'little inspirational rooms' with plenty of natural light, furnished with big boards for ideas posting, and wipe-clean walls. In Eindhoven, a monthly 'colloquium' takes place in a larger flexible space, providing a forum for teams to share ideas and inviting feedback, discussion and debate. When people are working on very confidential projects, 'Top Secret' spaces are created, usually tucked out of the way, to which only those working on the project have access.

ABOVE While most of the studio is open and spacious, there are pockets of project spaces where teams can hide away and create without feeling exposed.

LEFT The visual display of thought processes is important to Philips designers. In Hong Kong, glass, back-painted white, turns an entire wall into a place for sharing ideas.

LIVING BREATHING SPACE

Organisational change happens every six months or so at Philips Design, and the physical space is reorganised accordingly. Rooms are split in half, new areas discovered and temporary walls constructed. Over time, the spaces expand and contract in a most organic way, simple layouts allowing the space to be changed easily. The size and content of studio spaces is dictated by the pulse of work and scale of a project – with products ranging in physical size from a bedside table lamp to a full-scale MRI scanner. As appropriate and relevant for different projects, design teams create simulated spaces or areas that are used as backdrops to gain insights about users and further develop designs. These changes in the physical space fulfil the constant need to improve or change as a common trait of a designer or innovator. As Stefano Marzano, CEO and Chief Creative Director, puts it: 'Change is the constant thing in life.'

BELOW LEFT A Renaissance organisation: mixing traditional consumer products experience with fashion, textiles and other design disciplines supports big future thinking.

BELOW An on-site model shop allows quick prototyping of ideas, no matter how big or small.

RIGHT The simple form of a conference room table is brightened with recycled wood texture and a splash of colour.

EXPLORATION AND DISCOVERY

A large part of Philips Design's activity looks to the future. 'Next Simplicity' is a programme of work that looks at products that might be a few years away, while 'Design Probes' is a dedicated 'far-future' research initiative. Based in Eindhoven, the spaces that house these endeavours are surprisingly low-tech, looking more like a fashion college than the lab where the future of food, clothing or sustainable environments is being invented. Relaxed environments like these are just the thing people need when they're exploring ideas and playing around with things that do not yet exist. If you take the time to really look, the Design Probes team can be found on the top floor, through the café, up some dark stairs and behind heavy grey curtains. The team used to have a project space in the main studio, a glass box where they would collate research and develop ideas. However, it 'felt like being in a goldfish bowl. It was very uncomfortable, we felt self-conscious,' says Jack Mama, Creative Director. Now, hidden away in a lofty corner of the building, the space feels more like the turret of a castle, with a view that peeps through a small window. A more subversive space, it allows for exploration and play, free of criticism and challenge.

Philips designers look for 'good, honest, working, sensible solutions,' says Dirk Vananderoye, a Senior Product Designer at the Eindhoven studio. The philosophy applied to the design of the products Philips designers create for the outside world applies to their own world inside. The Philips Design spaces work. For such a renowned group of thinker-designers the spaces may appear to be rather simple, but once you pause a while and dig deeper, you realise that this simplicity is extremely well considered and thoughtfully applied. With sense and simplicity at the heart of what they do, these spaces have been conceived as such, allowing for evolutionary changes along the way. And the spaces will continue to change, because the creative endeavours of their nomadic occupants demand it. Great creative spaces: simple and flexible.

RIGHT The future-thinking Design Probes space is nestled high in a forgotten corner of the Eindhoven building.

PROCTER & GAMBLE

THE CLAY STREET PROJECT, CINCINNATI, OHIO, USA
SESSION FLOOR SPACE DESIGN: DAVID KUEHLER, DIRECTOR THE CLAY STREET PROJECT, 2004
STAFF OFFICE SPACE DESIGN: DAVID KUEHLER & LEAH SPURRIER, HIGHSTREET DESIGN, 2007

THE ATTIC, GENEVA, SWITZERLAND
DESIGN: JASON SHAW, P&G DESIGN MANAGER, OCTOBER 2007

PROCTER & GAMBLE is a Fortune 100 company that manufactures a wide range of consumer goods, organised into three categories: Beauty & Grooming, Health & Well-Being and Household Care. Founded by candlemaker William Procter and soapmaker James Gamble in Cincinnati, Ohio, in 1837, it is one of America's stalwart home-grown corporations. It now has approximately 135,000 employees in 86 countries, with its global headquarters in downtown Cincinnati. As befits such a large organisation, P&G's head offices are imposing in style and mass. Designed by Kohn Pedersen Fox in the 1980s, the towers dominate their own plaza, in a rich Art Deco, Post-Modern style with lavish veneers.

ABOVE Procter & Gamble's portfolio of products includes over 20 billion-dollar brands.

OPPOSITE An energised team prepare for a creative session in 'the Attic' at P&G's European headquarters in Geneva.

RIGHT A renovated brewery provides a spacious and affordable backdrop for the opening of minds and creation of ideas.

Perhaps counter to this corporate face, P&G remains dedicated to innovation. In 2008, it ranked number four in *Fortune*'s 'Most Admired for Innovation' list, and number seven in *Business Week*'s 'World's Most Innovative Companies' list. Having more than doubled the number of billion-dollar brands in its portfolio since the beginning of the decade (from 10 to 24), and with over 20 brands that generate between $500 million and $1 billion, P&G is a consumer goods powerhouse that has a clear lead in its market.

P&G is well known for its commitment to innovation. Welcoming external contributors through its 'Connect-and-Develop' open-source innovation strategy, the company has transformed its traditional in house Research & Development approach into a powerful method that embraces networks of external inventors, scientists and suppliers – which serves to fulfil its goal that around 50 per cent of new products are in some way initiated outside P&G's laboratories. This flexible, open thinking has radically changed the way P&G, and indeed other organisations, do business. And P&G's creative approach to business doesn't stop there.

The 'clay street project' is one of P&G's most unconventional answers to the challenge of generating truly breakthrough innovation; it's an off-site ideas incubator with a difference. Its aim is not only to provide the forum for new ideas, but also culture change. And it all takes place in a renovated brewery, in a run-down part of Cincinnati about a mile away from the global headquarters in the Central Business District. The choice of location is all part of the plan that former engineer, designer and theatrical producer David Kuehler and his team devised, in order to change the mind-set, behaviours and therefore the resulting innovation that comes from the brave groups who go through the clay street experience. By displacing employees away from their comfortable, predictable daily environments, the rule book is rewritten, and new ways of looking at the world are created. It was a tough fight to initiate, Kuehler, Director of the project, recalls: 'Taking people offsite, and *downtown* was the hardest thing I've done for the good of P&G.' It was not until Claudia Kotchka (former Vice President for Design Innovation and Strategy) and Kathleen Dalton (HR Associate Director of Design) walked the street themselves to see the new space, that the mythology of 'downtown' was challenged. And for P&G, a new place to innovate was born.

ABOVE P&G's clay street project location was deliberately chosen to take people out of their corporate comfort zones.

BELOW P&G's imposing headquarters in downtown Cincinnati, Ohio.

A PLACE TO NURTURE AND GROW

Kuehler joined P&G to set up a new global innovation programme after his partnership with Ivy Ross in Project Platypus – a ground-breaking product development initiative at Mattel Toys that led to the rejuvenation of the Barbie™ brand. Given this experience, Kuehler knew that an off-site location, where people would be exposed to new ways of thinking, was necessary and built the perfect space with the perfect process.

The clay street venue is reserved for serious innovation. Small groups of multi-disciplined people are taken away from their day jobs for up to 12 weeks to focus on a significant business challenge. This timeframe equates to a typical USA maternity leave: colleagues back in the business can pick up the slack for that amount of time, knowing that their co-worker's return is imminent. That the clay street project provides a protected, nourishing and nurturing environment where ideas are born is no coincidence.

BLACK-BOX THEATRE

Kuehler's experience in the theatre plays a large part in the clay street philosophy. Session areas are based on the concept of black-box theatre, which usually consists of a large square room with black walls and a flat floor. In other words: a simple, relatively unadorned performance space, where actors can quickly set and re-set the stage as needed, and the audience is focused more on the content of the performance than the design of the stage itself.

This principle resonates throughout clay street. A restored space of bare-brick walls, blackboard-painted areas, empty shelves and flexible furniture: this is a blank canvas upon which people can create. Ideas injected throughout the session quickly fill the walls with imagery and stories, and the in-house facilitation team clears away all evidence at the end of a workshop to allow new teams to start afresh: 'It doesn't matter what's happened before – it's up to you!,' says Michael Luh, the clay street project facilitator. While bare, the space is still comfortable. Flooded with natural light, there's a well-stocked kitchen, somewhere to pack personal belongings, access to the Internet and an abundance of supplies. The space is highly functional, its furnishings and details providing clues for behaviour. Big boards on wheels, stepladders and see-through bins full of Post-its®, sticks of glue, scissors and PLAY-DOH™ signal that this is a room for experimentation and creativity.

BACKSTAGE

The 'behind-the-scenes' areas are where the preparation happens – and where the facilitators find inspiration. This is where events and activities are conceived, designed to build the team's sense of security, honesty and worth, while developing a confidence for creative freedom and expression. These can include anything from an 'Improv' session, to a visit from a Chinese face reader or water connoisseur. Much of this planning happens during the two months prior to the team's arrival, and is executed during the project, with facilitators tailoring conditions rather than following any set formula. This creates a situation where comfort zones are stretched and mind-sets challenged, Michael Luh remarks: 'The part that scares most people is that we don't have an exact process but let a team's routemap emerge from the culture that they create and the problem at hand.'

The environment in which the facilitators design and plan a clay street journey is itself inspiring and stimulating. The 'womb' is a quiet space for research and reflection. Separated from the main space by bookshelves and a beaded curtain, the womb feels secluded and cosy, yet remains a part of the main space – a safe place where ideas for sessions are born. Black and white photographs from previous sessions are sentimentally displayed on the walls in family-style picture frames to remind the staff every day of whom they serve. For the clay street project facilitators, it's as much about the personal transformation participants undergo by the end of a session as the resulting business ideas.

ABOVE The project planning room, separated from the workshop studios, provides space for facilitators and managers to clearly define each clay street challenge.

OPPOSITE RIGHT At the beginning of any clay street session, participants are greeted with empty walls and boards on wheels. Custom-made equipment and furniture promotes 'off-the-shelf thinking'.

OPPOSITE LEFT 'The womb' sits on the third floor, in the heart of the facilitators' area. Stimulating books inform clay street session planning.

START-UP MENTALITY

While the main studio spaces are purposely bare at the start of any clay street project session, subtle yet provocative objects and considered details are included to encourage specific mind-sets and behaviour in the team. Much of the furniture and art is found and refurbished, or made from scratch by the clay street project facilitators.

Architectural details revealed during refurbishment are returned to their former glory and celebrated, providing a stark contrast to most corporate environments and a powerful message: innovation isn't about expense, it's about looking at things differently. 'We don't spend lots of money on the spaces — people get to discover that creativity can be born out of intentional constraints,' says David Kuehler. Artefacts salvaged from the cellar of an abandoned foundry stimulate curiosity, inspiring deeper thought. 'We want the participants to come into the room and be inspired by everything they encounter,' David explains; 'We want them to think, "Why is this here? Where did it come from? What's its story?"'

The scarcity of 'permanent' objects in the studio space shifts team members' minds to entrepreneurship. Participants of a clay street project are forced to think differently about how they do everything, from planning the project to deciding who will lead the team, through to finding ways to pay for consumer research groups. Rather than spending the usual several thousand dollars for a focus group, teams are given a limited budget and challenged to make it work. While the facilitators initially provide much of the structure and the input at the beginning of the project, the rest of the process emerges from the team.

LEFT This cosy retreat is created from an arrangement of shelving and beaded curtains suspended from the ceiling, creating a private yet inclusive space for focus.

OPPOSITE As a session unfolds, walls, shelves and tables swell with objects, pictures and findings that inspire the project team.

DIY, NOT OFF-THE-SHELF

A week before the session begins, participants receive hand-crafted starter kits which are stuffed with thought-provoking articles and objects. Assembled by the facilitators, these convey the subtle yet powerful message that time, care and attention goes into details that are normally take for granted. When things are not as they'd expect, the participants are forced to stop and think. Michael Luh explains, 'Everything is customised and intentional – we stimulate people not to take things for granted.' At the clay street project, nothing is off-the-shelf, since, as David Kuehler states, 'we don't ask participants for off-the-shelf ideas'.

The spaces are filled with simple and inexpensive solutions – such as flexible ideas boards, made from Homasote® on casters – reinforcing the message that here, it's all about creation. Since the team lives in the space for the entire 12 weeks' duration of the project, a sense of ownership and pride for their environment and the things they fill it with is cultivated.

FOUR YEAR DECLINE TURNED AROUND FOLLOWING CLAY STREET SESSION

2000 2001 2002 2003 2004

ABOVE 'Wish pots' represent the convergent and divergent thinking experienced at the clay street project.

RIGHT The clay street facilitators keep photographs of previous sessions as mementos.

ABOVE AND RIGHT Essential kit for clay street.

A. Open shelves display see-through bins full of supplies.

B. An abundance of Post-its®, tape, modelling clay, colourful pens and other essential creation kit.

C. Furniture cast on wheels provides flexibility for each group.

D. Curtains act as partitions allowing teams to change their 'set' as necessary.

E. A planet gong aurally punctuates gatherings and sets the tone for sessions.

F. Rugs are used to create visual boundaries for meeting areas.

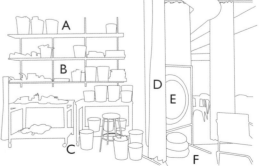

FROM SCARCITY TO ABUNDANCE

While a sense of scarcity gets people thinking like entrepreneurs, there are also pockets of abundance. Mesh bins overflow with supplies; magazines from near and far colour the shelves and walls. Highly visible, this communicates to participants that they should not skimp as they explore and develop ideas.

Another powerful tool that creates the right frame of mind for clay street participants is the presence of planet gongs that are dotted through the studios. Used for calling teams together for impromptu gatherings or signalling the start and end of exercises, they set the tone for each activity. Tuned to different frequencies, they are reputed to summon planetary energies: will, power and strength from the sun, grounding and stability from the earth, while Mars inspires passion, self-mastery and courage.

No two sessions at clay street are the same. While simple principles forge a safe yet challenging environment where teams and individuals can create, there is no linear set process. This requires a level of trust from senior executives, who can enter a programme mid-session to find what can only be described as chaos. However, once the stage is set and foundations of trust are built, a mind-set shift is achieved, and magic happens. The magic that's created at clay street is impressive – little over 18 sessions there have seen, among others, a reinvention of the Herbal Essences hair care brand (reversing a four-year decline in sales), the invention of a new product line (Swash, a re-wear laundry product for 'not-quite-dirty' clothes aimed at college students), and the reinvention of the global Pampers® nappy brand.

The clay street project has had a profound effect not only on P&G's business, but also on the participants. At the completion of a session, clay 'wish pots' are given out as part of a ceremony to capture the experience. Notes written by team members are placed inside the pots as 'well wishes', and alumni are encouraged to take these back to the business so that in times of need they may be drawn upon as reminders of new friends and a journey of self-discovery and growth.

Like the people who attend its sessions, the clay street project has also been on its own journey of self-discovery. 'I think we've changed our business model five times since we launched. We're always learning, always adapting,' says David Kuehler. Another important principle is that at the clay street project the sum of the parts is greater than the whole. 'No one person is as smart as all of us', explains Kuehler. Inside the creative space it is the staff members who have helped shape the experiences transforming P&G's people and business. Luh and Kuehler both agree that eventually they will have to step aside to allow for a new adaptation to emerge within their own staff. Luh expands: 'A new hybrid is just around the corner; we just need to get out of the way.'

THE ATTIC – A TOUCH OF THE CLAY STREET PROJECT ON-SITE

The Attic is P&G's latest innovation facility – an on-site space in P&G's Lancy Innovation Center in Geneva that borrows the principles and learning from the clay street project, applying them to ongoing issues. Like the clay street project, this is a place where certain rules apply. Corporate behaviours are left at the door, and a sense of play, fun and exploration is encouraged to solve tough business problems. Sabine Lucas, the curator of the Attic, is given full-time responsibility to manage the space. She takes great pride in protecting the environment, and ensures that users of the Attic respect the 'No *normal* meetings here' mantra. The understanding that creative thinking requires a creative space is so intrinsic here, that the Attic's diary is fully booked over three months ahead.

With floor-to-ceiling windows atop a five-storey complex in Geneva, the Attic boasts mountain views and an open rooftop garden; it is a popular place for taking in some fresh air and sunshine. Even on the brightest of days the space is well shaded by external steel slats, keeping the temperature down without compromising the view. Key furnishings and essential kit make this a flexible space; folding tables, chairs and boards – all set on casters – are in constant readiness for action. Set against an unassuming palette of grey, brightly coloured beanbags and art materials suggest that play and exploration is

ABOVE An outdoor patio provides welcome respite and a blast of fresh-air inspiration.

LEFT The Attic boasts uninterrupted views of the Alps from its five-storey perch.

permissible here: it's OK to make a mess! Post-its®, rough sketches, torn pictures from magazines, reused plastic bottles and card tubes forming 'low-res' prototypes are all part of the intentionally loose way of working here.

Yet this extreme flexibility is structured to ensure that all output from Attic workshops has direction, meaning and impact for the business. Sessions can run from one to several days and they address challenges and problems that require quick results. Designers and their cross-functional counterparts receive extensive training to run sessions here, their goal to create a structure within which people can step away from BlackBerries® and email to explore ideas very quickly and without constraint.

TOP Set against an industrial palette of stainless steel and grey, flexible furniture and colourful materials permit play and exploration.

ABOVE This clock injects a fun way of balancing the creative madness, ensuring timely results are achieved.

DROP BY DROP ... EMBEDDING CREATIVITY
IN THE ORGANISATION

While the clay street project and the Attic are reserved for teams solving specific issues on well-defined projects in a creative manner, many lessons have begun to seep into the fabric of the rest of the organisation on a day-to-day basis. 'Design thinking' and creative attitudes have started to become a way of life at P&G. Walking through the corporate offices you'll see informal meetings held in the many café-style areas that are scattered throughout the buildings. It's not unusual to see a dog taking a nap at the foot of its owner, a person snoozing in a metro pod, or a hairdresser giving a demonstration in the salon mock-up in the hair care department.

At P&G a genuine belief is rippling through the organisation: that if you want to change how well you're doing in business, you have to change the way you're doing business; that the environment matters; that creating an open, collaborative and safe place for people to explore, play and challenge is the key to unlocking creativity in people.

ABOVE TOP In the Geneva office, MetroNaps 'EnergyPods' provide a moment of uninterrupted relaxation: P&G embraces the power of an afternoon nap not only for 'fatigue management', but for inspiration and problem solving.

ABOVE It's not unusual to find a dog taking a nap at P&G's headquarters.

LEFT Café-style informal seating can be found throughout the P&G corporate offices in Geneva, encouraging casual meetings and impromptu exchanges.

SONY

SONY DESIGN

SONY ELECTRONICS DESIGN CENTER, SANTA MONICA, LOS ANGELES, CALIFORNIA, USA
INTERIOR DESIGN: GEORGE YU, 2007

SPRINKLER systems cast rainbows across emerald lawns surrounding this Art Deco-inspired office block in Santa Monica, the unlikely home of Sony Design's Los Angeles office. Tinted windows shield the occupants from the California glare, while a grand lobby and carpeted hallways offer no clue to the industry inside. Beyond heavy doors lies an open-plan design studio: clean, sparse and shining heavenly white. Here, new life breathes into Sony's newest design team, with a fresh way of working and a new space to create in.

The SEL Design Center, Los Angeles houses the product design team within US Sony Electronics, Inc. The Sony Design group has over 200 members worldwide including product, interaction and graphic designers with offices in Japan, England, Singapore, Shanghai and the United States. Created in 1961, the group designs over 2,000 products in a typical year. In addition to proposing product design concepts for the North American market, SEL Design Center, Los Angeles often collaborates with offices in Tokyo and Europe.

ABOVE Sony XEL-1, designed by the Sony Design Group, is an organic light-emitting-diode television with a 3-millimetre thin screen.

OPPOSITE Keeping things visually clean, simple and basic helps Sony designers to think from scratch.

Co-founded by Masaru Ibuka in 1946, Tokyo-based Sony Corporation was a ground-breaking company. Ibuka was a practical visionary who led Sony to create new and unique products that sheered from the Japanese corporate tradition of merely copying technology and ideas from the West. His ability to foretell how emerging technologies could be relevantly applied to daily life led Sony to build the world's first transistor television set in 1960, and to invent the legendary Sony Walkman in 1979. Ibuka also fostered an exciting working atmosphere and an open-minded corporate culture, another 'first' for Japan. In the founding prospectus, he wrote of his wish to build a company whose employees gained satisfaction and pleasure from their work and of his desire to create a fun, dynamic workplace.

FRESH NEW START

In February 2005, Sony's two North American design studios, based in New Jersey and San Francisco, were merged to form the new Design Center in Santa Monica, Los Angeles. Organised into four core groups – Product Design, Interaction Design, Visual Communication Design and Design Strategy – the LA Design Center is responsible for creating new products that not only exploit emerging technologies, but also tap into its own expanding library of music, movies and games to define new consumer lifestyles. The decision to move to LA was threefold: locating closer to Sony Electronics HQ in San Diego, where marketing, R&D, engineering and manufacturing facilities are based; being in the media and entertainment hub of Los Angeles, in close proximity to Sony Music and Sony Pictures; and having a space where the different disciplines for designing new products could co-exist.

The two-hour drive from the HQ to the Design Center provides 'good thinking time'; the two facilities are intentionally close but not too close. The space is reserved for creativity without too much influence from other Sony business groups, and 'surrounded by creative people who are thinking and behaving creatively,' says Alex Arie, the SEL Design Center's Director Industrial Design and Strategy. The Design Center is a place where a new team has been created, and with it a new philosophy. A protected realm, designers here are free from the pressures of business, affording creative autonomy and an opportunity to propose truly new things.

LEFT Untreated wood panels set against concrete floors create a raw yet warm tone for the space.

BELOW Deep, offset-hinged doors create a surprising and simple detail.

OPEN, NO BOUNDARIES

One of the first mandates of this new space was to communicate visually a very open, non-hierarchical approach to the way that the team does business, contradictory to corporate Japanese tradition. 'One of the most important things is that there are no boundaries between people,' explains Kei Totsuka, Senior Vice President of the Center. Uncluttered and open, natural light floods through windows on every side. Glass walls form private meeting spaces, while only two types of enclosed working space exist: project rooms which provide focus on ideas and a conference room where external partners come in and share confidential information.

As Sony designers are open to working with external companies, design teams, trend specialists and other interesting people, they have created space to accommodate these people too, as Arie explains: 'We place emphasis on the importance of connecting with different stimulus outside the company – we push ourselves to go out and bring in people who are interesting.'

Scattered throughout the studio are places to sit and chat informally: coffee points, a library stocked with magazines and inspiring books, and the 'virtual living rooms space', which resembles a family sitting room, and where designers are able to test their ideas in a home setting. It's clear that the space does not dictate how and when people should have ideas. 'Designers cannot switch off – they're always thinking, always having ideas,' says Totsuka. It's important, then, that the environment encourages people to relate to each other in a fluid way: 'It's not just about doing the job, it's about forging friendships,' states Arie.

This open and friendly environment embraces experimentation, whether of the space or in the space. Simple yet effective touches throughout make it an appealing place to create: tables are on wheels; desks are separated by movable panels; and huge whiteboards for hanging, pinning and sketching double up as space dividers – closed for focus or open for collaboration. The space is 'great and convenient for designing because you constantly have access to writing on walls,' says Parinaz Zamani, Visual Communication Design Manager; 'walls are so important – you write and erase and write and erase and take pictures of your thinking – it's all you need, you don't need to take notes any more.'

ABOVE Private 'Sake Box' project rooms are filled to the brim with ideas.

BELOW Sake Box exteriors break up the open studio and provide vertical pin-up space for communal information and inspiration.

BELOW RIGHT Designers huddle around a colleague's desk.

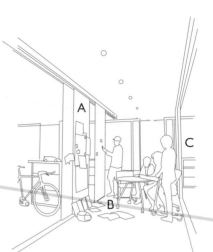

LEFT AND ABOVE A clean and functional flexible space:
A. Sliding magnetic whiteboard partitions allow teams to create space for projects, or enable individuals to close off to focus.
B. Furniture on wheels for quick rearrangement.
C. Personal storage units on wheels.

ABOVE Ideas and stimuli in thoroughfares encourage contribution. Magazines and journals from around the world are constantly refreshed and left on display to provide easy access to stimulus.

OPPOSITE Throughout the space there are opportunities to sit and browse magazines or books, or to chat with colleagues.

MY CUP RUNNETH OVER

Punctuating the main studio space is a wonderful approach to creative project rooms. The affectionately named 'Sake Boxes' are wooden, lidless boxes which offer vertical real estate on external walls for posting interesting notices, and a place within for ideas to brew. Providing space for longer-term focus, these are semi-permanent areas where information, insights and ideas gather and are displayed. These idea pods draw inspiration from the traditional Japanese sake ritual, where a cup is filled to the brim and allowed to overflow as sign of prosperity and generosity. This space is used beautifully for discovering ideas. The room is allotted to a designer, who uses it to explore an area of interest, concurrent to their day job. Having set their own agenda and agreed checkpoints with their manager, they fill the Sake Box with inspiration, artefacts, thoughts and observations. Over a period of about six months, the insights fill the whiteboard walls, literally forcing ideas to spill over the top. This is true exploration. The Sake Box provides the space for prolonged focus, without pressure; there is no limit to how many ideas can come from this – nor how 'finished' they are.

OPPOSITE A fully functioning 'living room' provides a contextual backdrop for new ideas.

BELOW Shelving is used to store books for reference as well as to define work areas.

CLEAN SLATE

The beautifully considered Design Center possesses an understated aesthetic that not only provides a blank canvas, it also appeals to the creative purpose ingrained in a designer's psyche. Cool grey concrete floors, whitewashed walls and exposed ducts, industrial corrugated metal ceilings and a warm untreated wood veneer combine to create a clean yet comfortable space. The use of raw materials is deeply intentional: 'If everything were processed and polished, then a designer's job is done,' says Arie. By connecting with the unrefined, the imagination is inspired to think of unlimited possibilities.

'Virtual Living Rooms' are areas in the Design Center that are used for testing their new ideas *in situ*. Exploiting their proximity to Hollywood, the designers use movie set props to furnish these spaces according to the target consumer's typical home environment. A Manhattan loft, family room or suburban kitchen can be mocked up to create contextual spaces that help the designers to think holistically. 'The mission of designers is not just the hard issues – it's about the context and the surrounding lifestyle,' explains Totsuka; 'Having a more holistic approach allows us to think bigger, so our space is an important reflection of that'.

The Sony Design Center in Santa Monica is a space where new working practices and environmental features have been prototyped to the benefit of the new team, and has also inspired other Sony Design Centers around the world. Designed by the late George Yu, a talented and respected architect who completed more than 65 projects which are characterised by his curiosity for and experimentation of technology, the Sony Design Center carries his legacy of exploration. Combining the simplicity of Japanese modern interior design and raw industrial practicalities, he has created a beautifully minimalist yet evocative result.

SONY MOVED FROM NUMBER SEVEN TO NUMBER FIVE IN RANK IN *GUIDE TO GREENER ELECTRONICS* RELEASED BY GREENPEACE IN MARCH 2009.

SONY MUSIC

SONY MUSIC

SONY MUSIC ENTERTAINMENT HEADQUARTERS, LONDON, UK
DESIGN: MOREY SMITH, 2008

SHARING the Art Deco facade of what was once Barker's department store, just around the corner from London's fashionable Kensington High Street and next to Richard Branson's exclusive Roof Gardens, Sony Music's UK headquarters radiates glamour. The thrill of its interior is discernible even from the street. The attention of passers-by is grabbed by the flash of the glossy mirrored black tiles in the vestibule reflecting distinctive pendant fluoro-tubes, and the sound of pulsating TV screens. Beyond this enticing welcome to the home of music entertainment is an upbeat yet relaxed, open workspace that challenges industry conventions and has opened up new, more collaborative ways of working.

ABOVE Sony Music Entertainment is the second-largest global record company of the 'big four' record companies and is controlled by Sony Corporation of America. Its record labels include Columbia, RCA, Epic and Syco, with signed artists such as Bob Dylan, Bruce Springsteen and Kings of Leon.

OPPOSITE The lift foyer of Sony Music Entertainment UK's London offices. An open industrial warehouse feel with touches of glamour creates a relaxed yet exciting atmosphere that befits the industry.

ABOVE A listed Art Deco building, this former department store off London's High Street Kensington is the new home for Sony Music.

ABOVE RIGHT A bespoke installation in the reception area streams energetic music videos non-stop.

OPPOSITE High-gloss black mirrored tiles, a four-screen video display and suspended fluorescent light tubes create a presence that can be seen from the street.

Sony Music Entertainment is the second-largest global recording company and a subsidiary of the Sony Corporation of America. Its origins date back to 1888 when its predecessor, the Columbia Phonograph Company, established the Columbia Records label. The oldest surviving brand name in pre-recorded sound, Columbia remains one of the most successful labels in Sony Music's fold. Several mergers and acquisitions mark Sony Music's history, the most recent being at the end of 2008, when Sony acquired Bertelsmann's 50 per cent stake in the company and became a wholly owned Sony business once again. Sony Music's labels include Columbia, Epic, RCA and Syco (Simon Cowell's entertainment label), with signed artists such as Beyoncé, Shakira, Leona Lewis and Kasabian. Many have received numerous awards, breaking records for longevity in music charts and record sales. Sony Music also runs one of the richest music catalogues in the world.

When designers MoreySmith suggested the huge open space that once operated as a department store shop floor, it took a leap of faith for Sony Music to proceed. The existing 97,000-square-foot deep, dark floor plates would require extensive structural work to become the home of music entertainment. MoreySmith's solution was to hide

storage and plant in a central core surrounded by communal spaces, with high-occupancy areas positioned around the perimeter of the building. Work areas that house almost 500 people are kept as open as possible, to allow natural light through and maintain visual connection with windows from practically anywhere in the building.

Sony Music wanted a contemporary space to reflect their relaxed, non-corporate style with an emphasis on open plan that still maintains the individual identity of each department. The resulting 'Music Emporium' achieves just that: a very collaborative atmosphere that doesn't dilute each label's autonomy or brand personality. In an industry where hierarchies are typically large and egos larger, where everyone from manager level up expects a separate office, this was a significant culture shock, and the in-house team and designers had a job to convince people about the benefits of opening up. While there were some genuine needs for privacy, such as listening to demo tapes, the opposition was largely habitual. Even with the full support of the company's Chairman, Ged Doherty, and some exciting virtual tours of the build, there was resistance right up to the move. But when people saw the new space, it was 'genuinely transformational', Emma Pike, Vice President Industry Relations, remarks. The space delivers on every expectation. Warehouse shabby meeting Art Deco chic, there is plenty of space to hang out, hold gigs, entertain and do business, while reassuringly private and public at the same time. A balance is struck between consistency and individuality with clever use of modular furniture, eclectic decorative touches, and a thoughtful workspace layout that provides departments with their own 'front door' while remaining linked 'backstage'.

OPPOSITE A double-height atrium opens up a café area and communal space that acts as a venue for daily lunches, whole-company meetings and full-blown gigs

BELOW LEFT Natural quirks in the building's floor plan are exploited to create semi-private nooks and kitchens while remaining connected to the main space.

BELOW AND MIDDLE Clever storage solutions manage creative 'mess' without inhibiting work styles:
A. Units arranged to form circulation routes that don't impinge on privacy.
B. Castellated units make space for display and filing while maintaining clean sightlines across the top surfaces.

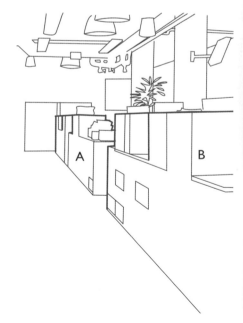

ABOVE Pivoting dividers open a team's workspace onto a casual meeting area. This double-height atrium area also houses a popular pool table.

OPPOSITE Diffused lighting and sightlines brighten the spacious atrium, which transforms from cafeteria and casual meeting space into the perfect muic gig venue.

IN THE FIRST YEAR OF ITS MOVE, SONY MUSIC BECAME THE NO.1 MUSIC LABEL IN THE UK AT BREAKING NEW DOMESTIC ACTS TO PLATINUM STATUS AND BEYOND. (FIGURES ARE FOR YEAR ENDING DEC 08.)

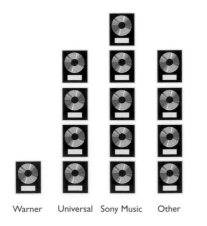

Warner   Universal   Sony Music   Other

Visitors arrive on the third floor to a vibrant and confirming welcome courtesy of suspended fluorescent tubes and a huge poster montage comprising bold album cover graphics. A bespoke AV system with 26 hidden projectors blasts music videos onto a suspended screen installation that 'gets the music out there' and dominates the spacious reception. Reclaimed pine floorboards, exposed structure, ducting and stencilled graphics amplify the lofty feel. Beyond the reception, the space opens out into two areas formed by two double-height atria that sandwich an inner core of the building's workings — kitchen, plant, WCs — and are connected by a ring of meeting spaces. The larger of the two atria is the hub of the building and site of the café, where staff have their daily breakfasts and lunches, and has become a place for receiving guests and for holding parties or company meetings. A balcony surrounds the spacious café and a bridge provides both quick access to the creative team and a great vantage point for watching gigs. In this, the deepest part of the building, the high ceilings, Barrisol® membrane diffusers and carefully planned sightlines create a sense of natural daylight. With dimmable lighting, rigging points to hang acoustic curtains and stage lights, spill-resistant concrete floors and a huge blank wall for projections, this is the perfect party venue. A mezzanine at the far end of the space, finished with vintage-style wallpaper and chandeliers, creates a cosy nook. Low-slung sofas and a chessboard coffee table make it a great retreat.

Surrounding this main space are two rings of meeting rooms, separated by glazing. Each space is furnished differently, reflecting a variety of meeting types: from casual and relaxing for listening to demo tapes, to more traditional for meeting suppliers or partners. Crittall™-glazed partitions provide an industrial yet elegant separation between the atrium spaces and the studio-style workspaces beyond. With their own individual entrance, each record label maintains a sense of its own territory; various colour, fabric and loose furniture options create individual styles, reflecting team identities. For example, the Columbia label area has bright red pivoting screens that open up onto a games space, but can be closed off to create a private work area.

Once inside the workspace, every department is accessible, linked by a circulation path created through furniture arrangement. The same basic furniture system is used throughout in various configurations and colourways, with a few exceptions. The creative team (responsible for album cover design, web and marketing materials) are the only team with contrasting furniture, big timber workshop benches signalling that they're 'a little different'. The team were also given a budget to furnish their space to their own taste. They came back with a horse.

Quirky nooks in the building that would otherwise be unwanted space are reserved for the HR functions and executives. Secluded, yet part of the overall workspace, a collaborative attitude is reinforced. Strategically placed screens and storage furniture obscures direct sightlines to the Chairman's space from the more public areas, which

also share the open-plan arrangement. There's no clean desk policy but a number of clever touches restrain the 'creative mess'. Partition units have whiteboards and colourful fabric offering pin-up space for fan mail and ideas on one side and space for storing TVs, hi-fis and accompanying paraphernalia on the other. Storage cabinets house memorabilia, awards, trophies and paperwork, with the castellated upper surfaces enforcing clear sightlines. Ceiling height is maximised where possible, with occasional suspended rafts concealing unsightly technology, lighting and environment services. Colours are kept fairly neutral, allowing the objects that inhabit the space to provide the decoration and the varied surface heights to add richness to the open space.

Sony Music's 'Emporium' has created a more unified feeling for the company while allowing teams to retain their individual identity. Sony's people have overcome preconceived fears of being out in the open, and this has had a dramatic effect: 'In the old building if you wanted to ask someone a question you'd have probably set up a meeting to talk about it, but here you just happen to bump into them or wander up to them and get the answer in two seconds – the effect it's had on time management and efficiency is incredible,' says Emma Pike.

Several collaborative initiatives have emerged since moving to the new offices, including a process innovation that aligns Finance, IT and the labels; a 'Sounding Board' group that acts like a parliament for staff, representing cultural aspects of working life at Sony Music; and an Ideas Scheme that has seen five individuals rewarded for implemented ideas in almost as many months. The space 'has taken a life of its own', says Mike Blacklee, Facilities Director, with parties, gigs and charity events not only saving big on venue hire, but also energising people around the work that is going on here.

With the music industry adapting to phenomenal change in the transition into the digital age and as it adopts new ways for people to experience music and entertainment, a whole new range of business opportunities is opening up for Sony Music. With many of these opportunities made possible through nurturing partnerships, 'having this space so that we can invite people here is fundamental!' says Mike Blacklee. The 'Music Emporium' is an uplifting, creative environment that accentuates Sony Music's vibrant and creative culture. It is a space the company is proud to bring visitors to and a space that, having challenged preconceptions of working open plan, encourages people to look to the future collectively.

ABOVE The creatives were given a budget for decorating their space. They came back with a horse.

OPPOSITE Sliding vinyl-padded doors offer a connection between a casual conference room and the CEO's open office.

T · · ·Mobile·®

T-MOBILE USA

!CREATION CENTER, SEATTLE, WASHINGTON, USA
DESIGN: GENSLER, 2007

T-MOBILE is a subsidiary of Deutsche Telekom (DT). Headquartered in Germany, DT is one of the world's leading innovative telecommunications companies. In terms of revenue, the United States represents T-Mobile's largest wireless market. T-Mobile USA currently serves more than 33 million customers. The company has pioneered new mobile phone features, such as myFaves which offers unlimited calls to your favourite friends and family. In 2008, T-Mobile also launched with Google the world's first Android smartphone – the T-Mobile G1 – providing customers with access to hundreds of cool and innovative applications as well as newly emerging mobile Internet capabilities.

ABOVE T-Mobile's Cameo digital photograph frame can receive images wirelessly from a smartphone.

OPPOSITE The open-plan library resource positioned adjacent to a high-traffic area for a spontaneous injection of inspiration.

ABOVE T-Mobile's !Creation Center is located in downtown Seattle.

ABOVE MIDDLE Inspiring product examples are displayed on floating plinths, with one left empty for T-Mobile's next creation.

ABOVE RIGHT A full-scale projection of new concept scenarios and provocative innovations, signalling that this is a place for big, new and exciting ideas.

OPPOSITE Quick access to both floors is facilitated by a spiral staircase, whose light construction adds to the open nature of the space.

Established in 2007, the !Creation Center is a bold experiment that pushes the boundaries of mobile communications, and rewrites the rules of how to operate as a business. A team of around 50 cross-disciplined people, including specialists in ethnographic research methods, rapid prototyping and big thinking, have made their home in downtown Seattle, 10 miles away from T-Mobile USA headquarters.

When it comes to really thinking outside the box, it helps to break out of the one that you're in, to get away from the walls that have been constructed around you – the very walls that define the world as you know it. For T-Mobile, in order to think really differently about how they create remarkable ideas that will 'jolt the mobile communications industry', they redefined their mission to focus not on technology, but on human relationships and a world where anything is possible. This new space supports a rebellious, non-corporate atmosphere, and with over 60 utility patents submitted for filing in its first two years of existence, the !Creation Center is proving to be a hotbed of intellectual property for T-mobile USA.

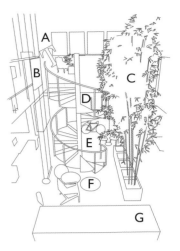

ABOVE AND LEFT T-Mobile's !Creation Center:
A. A freestanding illuminated 'T'.
B. A restored pulley system allows for quick transferral of large objects, such as ideas display boards, from floor to floor.
C. Double-height bamboo trees break the view and form a soft partition.
D. Spiral staircase.
E. People are encouraged to bring bikes to work.
F. Casual meeting areas are created adjacent to high-traffic junctions for impromptu chats.
G. A craft station in a centralised location.

BELOW A childhood poem printed on the spiral staircase is both wishful and inspiring.

JOLT TO THE INDUSTRY

Due to the fast-moving nature of the telecommunications industry, creating forward-thinking products and services was proving difficult to achieve, especially with much of the 'innovation' driven and controlled by the handset providers and tied to short-term product cycles. So in 2006, T-Mobile USA developed an advanced product and service design group, which focuses on delivering human-centred innovation and provides in-house consulting services. Rather than being limited to feature changes on phones, such as the inclusion of games and ring tones, this group allowed T-Mobile to break away from the usual way of doing telecommunications business and to branch out into offering products and services that enhance the way people communicate in their daily lives.

Headed by Joseph Ungari, Vice President of Advanced Product Innovation (and formerly of Philips, Whirlpool and Nike), the !Creation Center allows T-Mobile to take a bigger and more aspirational leap, controlling their product roadmap and driving innovation from the consumer's perspective. With the help of innovation consultants IDEO, Ungari quickly surrounded himself with an eclectic mix of highly talented and motivated designers, technology experts and consumer insight specialists. The primary purpose of the group was to develop long-term, 'remarkable' products that 'enhance personal relationships', something that was very difficult to do when ingrained in the day-to-day business back at the headquarters. In order to accomplish this, it was felt important to have a space where the atmosphere would be playful, exploratory, non-corporate, bold and brave – a space that would communicate, reflect and reinforce a new attitude and keep people pushing the boundaries. So they relocated from corporate headquarters to downtown Seattle, to a non-conventional studio on the top two floors of a non-conventional office block, with a recording of someone's dog barking for a door buzzer, a small organic coffee shop for an entrance, and a public art gallery for a neighbour.

Entering on the upper mezzanine, huge skylights fill the ceiling while the studio drops open before you. An abundance of natural light pours down to the workspace below, where the low false ceilings of corporate cube farms have been replaced by lofty double-height space and bamboo reaching skyward. Internal walls have been reduced to a minimum, cable balustrades maintain clear sightlines and quick access between floors is provided by a spiral staircase. The lobby surrounds you with an invitation to imagine future possibilities. Floating plinths display remarkable innovations from adjacent industries, with one left empty, waiting to be adorned by T-Mobile's next creation. A full-wall projection depicting possible future product scenarios offers clues to current thinking, while a new mission statement to guide them is placed virtuously high.

The top floor houses public, communal and team spaces. An open pantry, stocked with breakfast and break goodies, sits alongside a big kitchen table with bench seating. In

ABOVE The opportunity to write on walls, doors and windows is everywhere at the !Creation Center.

BELOW Whiteboard walls support the notion that ideas can be conceived – and captured – anywhere.

the far corner, a semi-private play area, dubbed the 'mosh pit', is equipped with the latest computer game equipment. Formal meeting rooms, casual spaces, LCD panels with news feeds, a reference library and a telescope spying on sailboats on the Sound complete the view. With large private offices banished, individual work areas are found on the lower floor, arranged in open plan and in the centre of the atrium. In close proximity to each other, these flexible workstations utilise small, movable tables, while comfy sofas and project rooms provide space for group work.

BELOW An automatic garage door offers a practical, flexible and fun partition between meeting rooms.

OPPOSITE Work desks are on casters to allow for easy layout changes.

RESPECTFUL REBELLION

Mavericks with a conscience, renegades within reason; the !Creation Center has struck a fine balance between being anti-corporate and remaining grounded in the reality of business. This space reflects that balance in many simple yet effective ways. Graffiti-covered walls, a lopsided giant 'T' sign, brightly coloured informal meeting spaces and lounging areas all make for a rebellious, non-corporate atmosphere. Breaking the rules is liberating and can release hitherto locked ideas. So a space that protects and supports non-corporate behaviour, as well as being flexible enough to provide familiarity to those who visit from the broader business, is an essential tool. Ungari enthuses: 'The spirit of anything is here ... and the space supports that notion.'

ABOVE Team project rooms have a working 'backstage' where the 'messy' work is done, and a 'veranda' area outside where ideas can be shared in a more controlled way.

ABOVE RIGHT A 'mosh-pit' gaming area is tucked away in a corner of the communal floor.

OPPOSITE An open kitchen with breakfast bar and large family table supports impromptu and casual meetings, and a small 'art gallery' showcases creations by !CC people.

60 PATENTS APPLICATIONS FILED IN FIRST TWO YEARS OF DESIGN CENTER

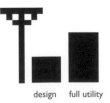

design   full utility

WRITING ON THE WALLS

At the !Creation Center, if you have an idea, you should be able to write it down anywhere – even on the walls. What is usually considered a forbidden act is encouraged; urban, youthful and irreverent, graffiti in this space signals that it is permissible to write on the walls too! There are blackboards for doors, whiteboards for walls, and even the glass can be scribbled on. Providing ample opportunity for thinking to be displayed encourages people to express and build their ideas. As a way of engaging and role-modelling this, the team 'tagged' their mosh-pit wall when they first moved in. Now, new members are initiated here.

DA VINCIAN PRINCIPLES – EXPLORATION, COLLABORATION AND SHARED THINKING

The !Creation Center is a place where learning is celebrated, exploration of materials, technology, history and sociology is embraced and experimentation is necessary. A craft workshop doubles up as a craft studio; a casual 'art gallery' displays personal work; and the open library offers not just printed matter but also objects, artefacts, live RSS feeds and other technology-enabled links to information – all supporting the group's belief in collaborative and exploratory Da Vincian principles. Project rooms are low-risk zones, allowing teams to share thinking and try unusual paths without having to pack information away every day. In these semi-permanent 'backstage' areas, the messy thinking of a project remains behind closed doors, while public 'on-stage' areas can be viewed from the passing corridor, allowing progress and outputs of the project to be easily communicated and reviewed by people outside the team. This happens regularly and can be anything from informal comments from passers-by to a more formal, considered presentation to the CEO of Deutsche Telekom for buy-in or sign-off.

By facilitating a culture of continuous feedback on formal, semi-formal and informal levels, ideas are always being shared and developed. This self-selecting environment of 'extreme collaboration', where ideas are always on display and people are always accountable and are constantly switched on, is not for the timid. It is a unique environment, and it suits a unique type of person. The !Creation Center looks for what IDEO calls T-shaped people: those who have a principal skill that's complemented by an empathy for and experience in lots of different things. Unlike the traditional engineering T-Mobile person, an ethnographic researcher, anthropologist or interaction designer brought into the !Creation Center might also be into welding, painting and motorbikes but not necessarily an expert in mobile phone technology. The trust and camaraderie developed when this diverse group of people work closely together means that ideas flow even after hours. Encouraging fun human touches in the environment cements these bonds. Toilets decorated by interns, the dog-bark doorbell and magazine cover parodies of team members – there are scores of playful touches throughout that reveal the friendly nature of !Creation Center people.

While the !Creation Center operates in a world of its own, with its own people and its own rules, it remains connected to its origins. The first step in taking the learning back to the main business is for the organisation to want to learn from these renegades, and in order to make that step easier, the space is intentionally welcoming. The T is respectfully returned to its upright position, a garage door separates 'informal' from 'formal', and people tuck in their shirts – 'just a little' – when external colleagues visit. Not in submission, but as a way of saying 'hey – we want you to be comfortable here too'.

URBAN OUTFITTERS

URBAN OUTFITTERS

URBAN OUTFITTERS, THE FORMER PHILADELPHIA NAVY YARD,
PHILADELPHIA, PENNSYLVANIA, USA
ARCHITECT: MEYER, SCHERER & ROCKCASTLE, LTD, 2006

WALK into any Urban Outfitters or Anthropologie store and expect to stay a while. The hip and edgy Urban Outfitters stocks bohemian, kitschy and ironic clothing and furniture, set against exposed air-conditioning ducts, raw concrete, steel girders and idiosyncratic architectural features. In Anthropologie, 'creative vignettes' have replaced clothing rails; an antique bed might serve as an anchor for displaying linens, towels, soaps and lingerie, or a birdcage house an array of diaries, jewellery and trinkets. The wares are always organised with layer upon layer of visual interest, and while no two stores are the same, they all share a common witty, eclectic and quirky sense of style. This left-of-centre approach to retail is core to the success of these businesses; it draws the consumer into an environment that appeals to their imagination and encourages them to explore.

ABOVE An Urban Outfitters storefront. Urban Outfitters Inc. owns affiliate brands Anthropologie, Free People, Terrain and Leifsdottir, a recently introduced luxury brand.

OPPOSITE Urban Outfitters' trademark use of found objects and eye for detail is drawn upon big-scale in the largest of five Navy Yard building conversions at their Philadelphia headquarters.

Richard (Dick) Hayne, founder of Urban Outfitters, Inc., opened the first store in 1970 near the University of Pennsylvania campus, and focussed on selling 'funky' fashion and household products to students. The company opened the first Urban Outfitters brand store in a converted warehouse in 1976, evolving the product line to appeal to a wider audience. The company has expanded over the years, establishing and growing affiliate brands Anthropologie, Free People, Terrain and Leifsdottir, a recently introduced luxury brand. The business revenue is now worth over $1.8 billion, thanks in no small part to a deliberate bucking of mainstream retail trends.

Until 2006, the Urban Outfitters companies were scattered across Center City, Philadelphia with disparate functions having little opportunity to experience the company as a whole. So when buildings within a decommissioned Navy Yard became available it offered more than just a large space where the business units could co-exist. It provided the opportunity for the restoration of a historical site in need of a big dose of creativity – a challenge that was compatible with the Urban Outfitters way of doing things and deeply appealing. Here was a dramatic space that could bind the teams physically, yet allow them to maintain creative autonomy.

The headquarters campus consists of five buildings, each with a strong sense of individuality, yet connected by a line of symmetry over four acres. Three are dedicated to the brands Urban Outfitters, Anthropologie and Free People, while one shares support functions with the new garden and outdoor furniture brand, Terrain, and a large communal building offers a food court, public cafeteria, library and gym. The aim, says David Ziel, Chief Development Officer, was to 'create the feel of one family with separate homes'.

TOP Each building that makes up the headquarters has its own personality. Materials are reused and preserved to retain the building's back-story, and found objects are used to furnish it.

ABOVE Naval ships still dock nearby. This awesome sight reinforces the industrial nature and scale of the campus.

RIGHT A decompression chamber found during demolition provides a delightfully industrial vignette.

BRINGING IT HOME

Unlike most retail chains, Urban Outfitters store layouts are not carbon copies of each other. Rather than creating a one-size-fits-all template, Urban Outfitters allows the space and architecture to dictate the store infrastructure and appearance. This approach to environment restoration pays respectful homage to a building's history, unveiling and celebrating authentic, latent beauty regardless of former use. Over 200 buildings – chapels, warehouses, banks, auto dealerships and cinemas – have been transformed into unique and inspiring stores, all with rich and complex environments consisting of a patchwork of layers designed to slow customers down, encouraging them to meander and providing time to soak up the detail. Urban Outfitters treats its customers to a creative experience in-store and extends this treatment to provide a creative experience in their employees' workspaces. By taking these principles – that respectful, rich and layered environments inspire people to think creatively – and threading them through the fabric of the workplace, Urban Outfitters has created not only a stunning place to work, but a new destination for the public to visit. 'The excitement created in store is replicated here,' says Bill Cody, Chief Talent Officer; 'people come here and are immediately struck by the beauty.'

ABOVE Mezzanines provide space for team meetings where collection reviews are made easy with a simple hanging system fashioned from steel wire fencing. Recycled tabletops and salvaged chairs add to the eclectic style.

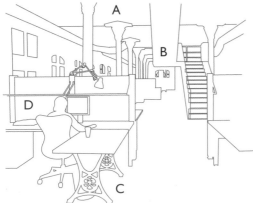

ABOVE AND LEFT A 'standard' Urban Outfitters workspace:
A. Ornate steel columns replace large wooden pillars that were removed to minimise fire risk but have been put to good use elsewhere on-site.
B. A set of stairs is halved and twisted through 180° to optimise light through the building.
C. Cast-iron table legs based on the old Singer sewing machine are custom-made with an Urban Outfitters design, although some original Singers can be found.
D. Work desks are based on a modular system that satisfies all 600 employees at the headquarters.

OPPOSITE Exposed ducts and ceiling supports: a timeless industrial backdrop for the design of vibrant patterns, sumptuous textures and vivid colours.

ABOVE A former acid bath becomes a beautiful fern garden.

BELOW Wooden pillars salvaged from one of the buildings are crafted into a breathtaking entrance in the shared services building.

BELOW RIGHT Teams chose their work area layout to include central communal desks made from reclaimed wood tops on trestle table legs.

ADAPTIVE REUSE

'Adaptive reuse' is a creative method of addressing sustainability issues with obvious cost benefits. By identifying how something may be adapted, reused, refurbished or refigured, not only are natural resources saved and energy consumption reduced, but an appreciation of the life cycle of man-made objects is also developed. Urban Outfitters embraced adaptive reuse before the phrase became trendy, tapping into the behaviour of its target market of students, who would take old traffic signs and turn them into a coffee table, or fashion a bar stool from a tractor seat.

This philosophy has fuelled a multitude of creative solutions and whimsical additions to the working environment over and above the restoration and preservation of the buildings themselves. An acid bath is transformed into a fern garden, former wood columns become a grand staircase, and an abandoned decompression chamber has new life as a sculptural piece between buildings. Workstations are custom-built using replica I-beam sections of those reclaimed from the demolition, while concrete desks have Singer

sewing machine-inspired cast-iron legs. At a fraction of the cost of standard office desks, two configurations satisfy all 1,000 employees. The 'standard' workstations, for all support functions, make use of the home-built work surfaces with side tables made from reclaimed wood. The 'creative' workstations (for merchants and designers) share the same desking system, but have additional communal areas for design work and showcasing new collections. Both are configured in clusters according to the team's needs, and are defined by Homasote® recycled paper walls which provide pin-up space for concept sketches, materials samples and mood boards, and are strong enough to support shelves and clothes racks.

Outside, the creative recycling continues. Old rail lines define pathways between buildings, while 'hard waste' from the demolition has been put to great reuse. Defective terracotta tiles, concrete and asphalt have been crushed and mixed to create attractive mulch. Affectionately named 'Betty Rubble', this is scattered between huge slabs of 'Barney Rubble' paving material, forming a decorative and functional water drain around the buildings. The entire campus exudes the joy of discovering new uses for old things and reinforces a cultural characteristic that is intrinsically creative.

ABOVE The main corporate functions are co-located in a building that reflects a timeless, more 'classic' style of reuse, paying attention to neutral tones.

GROWTH IN ANNUAL EARNINGS INCREASED FROM AN AVERAGE OF 27.5% SINCE URBAN OUTFITTERS WENT PUBLIC IN 1993, TO 31.2% WHEN THEY MOVED TO THE NAVY YARD IN 2007.

A JOURNEY, NOT A DESTINATION

In the Urban Outfitters retail environment, people are taken on a journey that draws them in, tickling their imagination and lulling them into a creative state. This piques curiosity and implies constant movement rather than a finite point of completion. The 'unfinished' nature of these spaces is a critical part of the underlying creative philosophy: 'If things are finished, then you've nowhere left to go,' Hayne explains. Paint peeling from columns, untreated sealed walls, partly sanded floorboards — it's all about continuing a journey, not about having arrived. For Urban Outfitters, 'there is no static state ... except the final'. In other words, stop creating and you're dead.

Awash with the patina of time, the workspaces are like an archaeological dig with layers of history, use, misuse, construction and man-made creativity that peel back to expose stories and engage the imagination. Hayne explains: 'When you see the layers of time, your mind fills in the gaps. It says "I wonder what that was, what those layers of paint have seen in their time, who did that, and the next thing – who's going to paint it, because obviously it needs it!" We find this kind of thing exciting – it implies curiosity, imagination, stories.' Not only does the non-treatment of materials leave a blank canvas for the designer's imagination to work upon, there's something in the basic, raw, industrial materials that makes them unaffected by trends. 'Finishes will go out of fashion, as will colour, but raw materials such as concrete, wood, metal etc will not,' says Ziel; and given the nature of the business that Urban Outfitters is in, the timelessness that comes with this environment has a grounding effect for designers.

TOP Throughout the buildings there are hundreds of opportunities to form impromptu huddles, hold private phone calls or relax, with no two areas looking the same.

ABOVE The company's free gym sits on a mezzanine level above a glass-fronted boiler room.

LEFT The Urban touch: damask wallpaper in relief used to line a concrete mould creates a beautifully subtle pattern.

FAR LEFT Former rail tracks are now used to define pathways around the campus. The celebrated I-beam houses path lighting, set into 'Betty Rubble' and 'Barney Rubble': mulch and paving slabs from the demolition.

OPPOSITE All flooring is reclaimed, often coming from unusual places such as basketball courts and even a convent.

SCALE

Set against this great attention to detail is a backdrop of colossal scale. The largest, most challenging, yet ultimately fun space that Urban Outfitters has created to date is the building that is home to the communal areas. Here, and with Mandelbrotian beauty, the tiny is juxtaposed with the enormous. Stepping into this space, your eyes are drawn from hand-scattered reclaimed green glass inclusions embedded in the floor up ... and up ... to the lofty heights of the ceiling. Giant shipping ropes hanging from gantries like Brobdingnagian thread, a naval chain that evokes a gargantuan discarded necklace, and oversize chairs, all make you feel as small as an ant. Fifty-five-foot-high windows frame the working dock, where active ships bolster the scale and emphasise the industry of the place. Huge pipes and functioning centrifugal pumps, which heat and cool four of the buildings, are set behind glass, revealing the innards of the campus. High above, on top of the pump room, tiny joggers appear to run on air as they work out on the gym mezzanine that shares the cavernous ceiling. Hayne has embraced the scale, recognising its ability to engage people when he says: 'By paying respect to a space and working with scale, the entrance and the experience of a building you can inspire people.' Inspired people make creative people, and at Urban Outfitters they have them in droves.

Urban Outfitters' move away from the bustling Rittenhouse Square in Philadelphia's Center City was a bold one that brought with it a few cultural challenges, including how to keep a collection of creative people, who thrive on external stimuli, engaged. The former Navy Yard is arguably one of Urban Outfitters' finest creations, whose fabric is stimulating and filled with undiscovered stories. Truly inspiring, the respect that is paid to the buildings, from the minute details to the imposing scale, is so compelling that not only do people love to work there but the public makes the effort to visit too – and neither mind staying a while.

VIRGIN

VIRGIN MANAGEMENT LTD, THE SCHOOL HOUSE, LONDON, UK
ARCHITECTURE AND INTERIOR: SPACELAB | GRAPHICS: HIM ME & HER, 2008

VIRGIN ATLANTIC, THE BASE, CRAWLEY, UK | DESIGN: UNIVERSAL DESIGN STUDIOS, MAY 2007

VIRGIN MEDIA HEADQUARTERS AND CUSTOMER CONTACT CENTRE, HOOK, HAMPSHIRE
AND WYTHENSHAWE, GREATER MANCHESTER, UK
DESIGN: HOUSEHOLD, 2007

Did you know ... ?
... that Richard Branson has been voted the most admired businessman, the most desired boss and the number one choice for a father? (Daily Telegraph, 2004; Talent2, 2005; Daily Telegraph, 2009)

VIRGIN GROUP is an international conglomerate of more than 200 privately held companies that combine to generate over $20 billion in revenue. The Virgin brand operates in a multitude of sectors ranging from mobile telephony to transportation, travel, financial services, leisure, music, holidays, publishing and retailing. While comprising many different businesses, Virgin's brand, visual identity and creative spirit is as evident in its call centres as it is in its Upper Class lounges. This disparate group of companies is bound together by a combination of Richard Branson's charismatic and visionary leadership and the Virgin brand personality.

ABOVE An Upper Class Virgin Atlantic bed. Virgin is a conglomerate of over 200 companies, tied together with a strong brand and spirited culture.

OPPOSITE The 'Love' meeting room at Virgin Group headquarters.

Entrepreneur Branson dropped out of boarding school at the age of 17 in 1967 to start his own magazine, *Student*, which was an immediate success and a surprise to his parents. His second venture, a mail-order record business, led to the opening of a chain of discount-price record stores, named Virgin Records, which formed the foundation for what would become the Virgin Group as we now know it, and as Branson calls it: 'branded venture capital'. Along the way, Branson has attained cult status as a result of his business exploits, quests for adventure, and unique personal style. A rebel by nature, Branson loves a good challenge and enjoys bucking convention. Often ridiculed for attempting to go into new industries despite no prior knowledge or experience in them, Branson came up with the 'Virgin' name as a tongue-in-cheek way of signifying his ignorance. But this ignorance has typically placed Virgin in a unique position; naïve eyes looking at often-tired industries, resulting in being able to identify opportunities their competitors would often miss due to sector preconceptions.

Virgin has become a 'way-of-life' brand – breaking all the conventional business and branding rules, trying out new business ventures, often surprising the industry and delighting consumers. As the group swells to include over 50,000 employees, the brand remains a critical engine for binding the businesses together with a common set of values, language and culture, with the environment as a vehicle that carries the spirit of one man to many.

VIRGIN MANAGEMENT LTD OFFICES

Virgin Management Ltd resides in a converted old school house in Brook Green, a leafy neighbourhood of West London. This 24,000-square-foot building provides plenty of space for the 100 staff to grow into, with room to welcome fledgling businesses into the fold. As corporate headquarters it houses the 'guardians' of the Virgin brand, Virgin Management Ltd, who act as consultants to new Virgin start-ups, with responsibilities that include PR, people and culture. They are joined by Virgin Limobike (a motorbike taxi service in London), Virgin Insight (an in-house database marketing company) and Virgin Unite (Branson's non-profit venture that focuses on social and environmental innovation).

Designed by Spacelab, a relatively young award-winning London-based architecture firm, the Virgin headquarters is made up of disparate teams working on individual goals. The building occupies a linear layout so connecting people both physically and through the brand became an important aspect of the space in order to promote creative ideas sharing and to continually fuel the energy and spirit of a cohesive brand personality and culture.

Entering through glass doors, the space delivers its first Virgin brand surprise: a greeting

TOP Headquarters: a provocative challenge references Branson's book and sets the tone of the business.

ABOVE Virgin Limobikes parked outside the Virgin headquarters in Brook Green, London ready for pick-up.

RIGHT Triggered upon entry, a greeting is projected onto the welcome desk at the London headquarters. Bold graphics in reception depict the breadth of Virgin businesses.

BELOW Headquarters: park benches and Britain-inspired graphics celebrate the company's heritage.

projected onto the reception desk – just for you. Bold graphics excitedly depict the range of industries that Virgin covers, and sexy lipstick red sets the heart racing. Three-foot-high words exclaim 'SCREW IT', referencing Branson's autobiography, *Screw It, Let's Do It*, and set the tone that has fuelled the company's success.

All around, vibrant images relay Virgin's history: a very British corner, complete with park bench and a red telephone-box wall vinyl against a backdrop of Buckingham Palace and the Sex Pistols. Ornate gilt frames mounted against exposed brick warmly display images and trophies, including gold and platinum records and the Virgin Records label's first logo design. Pop music playing throughout most of the building delivers a sensorial reminder of this heritage. Following a generous 'sweetie tube', whose candy dispensing points on every floor connect the spaces, the eye is drawn up through the three-storey atrium and past glass-walled meeting rooms

that are themed to represent the sentiment behind the Virgin values: 'Love', a cosy lounge with neon sweetheart and vinyl lipstick kiss; 'The Boxing Ring', signifying Virgin's commitment to fight for the consumer; and 'Innovation', a clean, predominantly white room with graph-print walls that invite ideas scribbling.

Progressing through the lower floor, meeting spaces are themed to represent the territories that Virgin brands operate in: 'Bondi', 'Bollywood', 'Ulusaba' and 'Manhattan' boast beach, the vibrancy of India, safari, and a spectacular skyline respectively. Further meeting spaces are dotted throughout the headquarters, each with unique visual identities, but all reflecting the Virgin personality. When booking a room, a 'random meeting generator' suggests a different meeting room each time in order to encourage people to explore different areas of the building and switch their environment wherever possible. While the reception area and some meeting spaces are energetically decorated to imbue the Virgin spirit, main working spaces have the graphics toned down. Functionally equipped with flexible desking systems that hide clutter and eliminate cable mess, these spaces are designed to support team focus and concentration. Each space has an accent colour that dominates one wall with a simple graphic reinforcing a relevant aspect of the brand.

Virgin's brand personality allows it to enter into hitherto dry, staid, traditional or clinical industries, approaching them with a human touch and sense of fun. Even the most 'serious' industries such as air travel, finance and health have been tackled in true Virgin style. One of Virgin's specialities is in 'making a serious point in a fun and engaging way', says Damian Schnabel, Head of Group Brand Creative, which has had an enormously refreshing and powerful effect: in-flight safety videos are watched, bank statements digested. Virgin's approach to its working environment is no different. They get the basics right first then layer on the sparkly touches with cheeky wit, honesty and a human manner which engages people and inspires in them a spirit that they can do anything.

VIRGIN ATLANTIC – 'THE BASE'

Virgin Atlantic is one of the world's leading long-haul airlines. Recently celebrating its 25th year, it has become a global brand through its unique customer experience and exquisite environment design. Its focus on delivering safety and function first, then value for money and then the unexpected has changed the way people experience air travel, from a seamless online experience, to limo pick-up and check-in en route to the airport, to the in-flight entertainment, to the cleverly designed flat beds and on-board bar area that have won countless product and service design awards. At every step of the journey where Virgin Atlantic is able to provide it, passengers receive the Virgin 'touch'.

'The Base' is Virgin Atlantic's facility that houses engineers, crew and 'back-of-house' staff all under one roof. A converted warehouse on an industrial park a stone's throw from Gatwick airport, this colossal 240,000-square-foot building accommodates up to 2,000 people over two floors. Designed by Universal Design Studios, who have a strong portfolio on fashion, retail and restaurants, the front-of-house areas at The Base were conceived to make business operations more efficient. This office space and training facility is beautifully designed and highly functional, providing the first experience of the Virgin Atlantic brand for new employees.

Upon entering what looks like an oversized shed, one is immediately surprised by beautifully maintained trees growing through the terrazzo floor, reaching past a backdrop of custom-designed 3D tiles up to an ingenious sky-lighting system that scoops natural daylight up and softly diffuses it through the space. With its high-design welcome and a corridor that delivers the 'red carpet' treatment, visitors are swept deep into the

BELOW The Base: the 'red carpet' leads directly to the heart of the 240,000-square-foot facility; a portrait of Virgin founder Richard Branson looks on.

BELOW RIGHT Located near London's Gatwick airport, Virgin Atlantic's The Base is a staff training facility with space for up to 2,000 flight staff and ground crew.

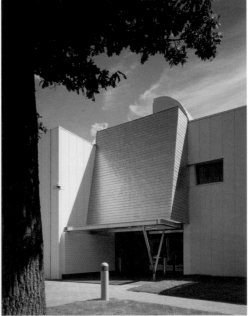

INTERNET & ATM

heart of the building, which feels more like stepping into an Upper Class lounge than an aircraft training facility.

Past security and a staff shop stocked full of travel essentials, one arrives at the 'Town Square' – a large communal space where everything you'd expect to see in a town centre can be found: a café, library, Internet point, ATM and travel agent. There is also, of course, a beauty salon good enough for a busy high street, which explains how Virgin Atlantic crew manage to keep up appearances! But there's one thing extra – there's a plane in the building! Respectfully displayed behind curved glass, a full-size cockpit, fuselage and row of check-in desks bring the core ingredients of commercial aviation into the communal space and the training room. Reminiscent of an airport viewing deck with floor-to-ceiling windows, the excitement of airport arrivals is evoked and here the majesty of flight is celebrated. A place for reconnecting with colleagues, the experience is enhanced by fun touches such as programmable message boards, through which co-workers and friends keep connected. This training facility includes manual and automatic check-in desks, galleys, every seating configuration the planes house, emergency doors,

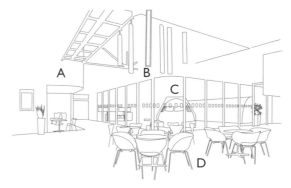

ABOVE The 'Town Square' at The Base, where flight crew and ground staff connect.
A. An extensive array of facilities include a café/bar, beauty salon, general store, library, Internet and ATM.
B. A programmable scrolling message board keeps colleagues in touch.
C. An aircraft cockpit, fuselage and check-in kiosks stand behind viewing glass.
D. Casual seating provides ample space to catch up.

ABOVE The Base: internal courtyards are created with exterior elements – trees, natural light and public seating.

ABOVE RIGHT A cone structure in one of the break-out spaces at The Base filters in natural light and provides an elevated coffee-break experience.

life rafts, emergency chutes. A further 50 or so training rooms are arranged in colour-coded clusters, around sleek break-out areas furnished with hardwearing seating and table arrangements that are softened by diffused natural light, curved forms and planting. Even deep within the belly of this enormous building, natural light is guided into classrooms through clever use of frosted glass-effect films.

At The Base, the same brand values that are bestowed on Virgin Atlantic's passengers treat its staff. It says: 'We're investing in this space because we're investing in you,' Joe Ferry, Head of Design explains. By investing in the staff and creating a truly extraordinary environment, Virgin Atlantic elevates their sense of worth and encourages them to deliver extraordinary service.

VIRGIN ATLANTIC DESIGN STUDIO AND MOCK-UP CENTRE

Adjacent to The Base, 'The Office' houses the corporate functions of Virgin Atlantic. Here, the Virgin Atlantic design team shares an open-plan studio area with quick access to 'expert users' (crew and ground staff) and the head space to explore concepts. Engineers and crew join the team at various stages throughout the process, contributing to 'blue sky' idea sessions without the 'it'll never fly' attitudes and bringing pragmatic experience to idea development. A nearby aircraft hangar serves as a mock-up centre, where several fuselages are squeezed in to allow full-scale prototyping.

VIRGIN MEDIA CUSTOMER CONTACT CENTRES

Virgin Media is Virgin's largest company, employing around 13,000 people in around 70 offices, and is headquartered in Hook, Hampshire in the UK. Formed in 2007 through the merger of ntl:Telewest and Virgin Mobile, Virgin Media became the UK's first 'quad play' media company, combining digital TV, super-fast fibreoptic broadband, home phone and mobile.

In a huge re-brand of the business, the overhaul involved rethinking and refreshing the organisational structure as well as the environment. 'The last thing you want to do is just stick a badge on the walls,' says Adrian Spooner, Creative Director at Virgin Media. Here was an opportunity to spread the Virgin culture throughout the newly acquired businesses. The strategy for the turnaround was to focus on the staff first, enabling them to focus on the customer, which will ultimately make the shareholders happy.

Focusing on truly affecting the people who are in touch with the customer daily, work started on three pilot customer contact centres where the day-to-day roles of the employees, whose average age is 23, include busy periods of customer calls. The buildings acquired from the former merger spanned a huge range of varying sizes, functionalities and states of repair, so a 'chocolate box' modular approach was taken to ensure brand consistency while allowing for individual quirks. Virgin Media appointed Household, a London-based firm that specialises in branded environments and retail design solutions, to humanise the call centre spaces, making people feel at home, feel free to be themselves and actually look forward to coming to work.

The theme 'Our Neighbourhood' was conceived, providing a visual language which now permeates through

BELOW LEFT The headquarters of Virgin Media presents a bold and energetic welcome.

BELOW Hedge-style bookshelves form partitions that flexibly define meeting spaces in Virgin Media contact centre areas.

the spaces creating a sense of ownership and empowerment for employees, as well as making them feel comfortable and at ease. 'With this concept, we could draw upon inspiration to make the spaces more homely,' says Spooner; so where there used to be peeling paint, you now have wallpaper, gilt picture frames and stencils depicting domestic objects – 'things you would not normally see in an office'.

The Virgin personality is expressed through a tone that befits this young audience. Bold and witty visuals encourage people to chalk up celebrity spottings on blackboard walls, and vinyl-covered MDF graphics suggest grandeur without costing a fortune. 'All these little touches don't cost a lot, but put together become really powerful,' says Spooner. These 'clever, human touches' have had a profound effect, positioning Virgin Media as fun and vibrant, internally as well as externally, and injecting the business with a creative passion that has seen retention levels soaring.

Branson's entrepreneurial spirit echoes throughout the environments at Virgin. 'Screw it, let's do it' rings out through the organisation, empowering people to do business the 'Virgin way' – focusing on the customer's experience, fighting the consumer's corner, daring to do it differently and doing it with a sense of fun. The environment is a key part of delivering the Virgin brand experience, acting as a conduit for expressing the brand personality, instilling a sense of self-worth and inviting people to feel comfortable, be themselves and ultimately help deliver the brand experience to delighted customers.

TOP Virgin Media: simple, inexpensive touches such as blackboard paint and graphic speech bubbles encourage interaction, individuality and a sense of fun.

MIDDLE Fun graphics greet arrivals in the car park of a Virgin Media contact centre. The coveted front-door spaces have been reserved to celebrate internal relationships!

FAR LEFT With over 90 Virgin Media facilities needing a facelift and the entire culture requiring a post-merger revival, attention was paid to high-traffic, communal areas.

LEFT High-impact floor-to-ceiling graphics and exposed light bulbs in the main reception at Virgin Media present a youthful and energetic message.

ABOVE Simple yet fun additions: a ladder is used to display newspapers beneath a silhouette graphic at a Virgin Media contact centre.

RIGHT Virgin Media: bold graphics provide an inexpensive hint of grandeur.

100%

80%

0%

IN AN INDEPENDENT SURVEY, OVER 80% AGREED THAT THE ENVIRONMENT WOULD HELP CHANGE THE CULTURE AND THEY COULD SEE A FUTURE FOR THEMSELVES WITH THE BUSINESS.

WALT DISNEY IMAGINEERING

GLENDALE HEADQUARTERS, CALIFORNIA, USA
1401 FLOWER STREET: IN-HOUSE DESIGN, 1960
THE BOWLING ALLEY: IN-HOUSE DESIGN, LATE 1980s
WDI R&D: IN-HOUSE DESIGN, PURCHASED IN 1997

THE brains and talent behind Disney Parks and Resorts, Walt Disney Imagineering (or as employees of WDI are called – 'imagineers') work closely with the Disney properties throughout the world, which include thousands of acres of land, 11 theme parks in five resort locations around the world, retail-dining-entertainment complexes, hotels and resorts, a private island in the Bahamas, and two cruise ships (with two more on the way). They are responsible for dreaming up new attractions, shows, environments and experiences, seamlessly delivering stories that delight and entertain their 'Guests'. Imagineering holds more than 100 patents in special effects, ride systems, interactive technology, live entertainment, fibreoptics and advanced audio systems.

ABOVE Walt Disney imagineers conceive and develop theme park attractions such as Expedition Everest.

OPPOSITE Dr Ben Schwegler, Senior Vice President and Chief Scientist, can be spotted riding his bike or scooter around the Research and Development department.

ABOVE Walt Disney himself still has a huge presence at WDI.

WDI is the result of Walt Disney's ambition to immerse people in the stories and characters that made Disney famous. He also wanted to inspire the imagination by making the impossible possible, so he conceived a theme park that would literally bring stories off the page and into a 3D environment. Originally a private company which was to merge into Walt Disney Productions, Imagineering remains the creative arm of Walt Disney Parks and Resorts, and is instilled with an entrepreneurial spirit and a mission to invent and reinvent how the world experiences theme parks.

Over 140 disciplines are shared by around 1,000 employees – from sculptors to rocket scientists, storywriters to architects, animators to mechanical engineers. The term 'imagineering' expresses how this melting pot of talented people work, reflecting the way they engineer imaginative experiences by dreaming big, before making those dreams a reality.

LEGENDS ON THE WALL

BELOW LEFT The original sketch for Disneyland by Herb Ryman was completed over a weekend and used to convince investors to back Walt's dream.

BELOW Walt Disney Imagineering headquarters in Glendale, California.

Stories and legends are powerful vehicles for communicating the history of a company, how it has grown, what has been successful and the types of behaviours that are admired by the business. For Disney, the culture of young and old, family values and visionary thinking are emblazoned on the walls. But it's not done in a linear fashion; you'll not find a company timeline posted in reception. Rather, exciting videos about new attractions as well as artwork, photographs and objects are proudly placed on display in high-traffic areas, providing vignettes that are at once inspiring and humbling.

The notion of legacy is very important at WDI, so rather than having new, custom-built spaces, Imagineering has created its home out of old warehouses and a disused bowling alley. The plot of land where WDI is now located was originally the site of Los Angeles' first airport, Grand Central Airport, which closed in 1959. Prudential later developed the property to create the Grand Central Business Center (GCBC), and WDI has occupied and bought several buildings over the years.

At WDI, environment is used as a storytelling tool to highlight and illustrate great people and great moments over the company's history – from Walt's original mission to create a place where families could lose themselves in a fantasy world, to the story of artist Herb Ryman's weekend sketch of Disneyland that helped sell the concept to New York investors. Everywhere one looks there are artefacts and artwork that connect the present with the past. Tributes are paid to the 'Disney Legends' of Imagineering, which include the late John Hench, official portrait artist of Mickey Mouse, who worked until the age of 95 and in whose honour a hallway has been dedicated with tributes by Disney artists. It's this sense of legacy – of great people having great passion to work tirelessly and with such talent – that is inspiring for present and future imagineers. Making these stories visible communicates to people that the business has come from somewhere inspiring – and that knowledge provides a strong sense that it's headed somewhere exciting. Nancy Hickman, Director, Creative

Development, describes it as 'nostalgic and forward-thinking all at once'.

One of the most revered spaces on the Imagineering campus is the Sculpture Studio which houses a vast array of three-dimensional works of art – from 12-inch-high bronze castings of Tinker Bell to monumental, two-storey steel and plaster constructions of *Jungle Book* characters Mowgli and Baloo. Nestled away in the main building, visitors experience a moment of peace and calm on entry before marvelling at the time, care and attention that is poured into each creation. Twenty-foot ceilings meet cabinets displaying work from generations of WDI talent. Faces of familiar characters peer down from shelves: crafted moments of life suspended in time; the space is a culmination of layers, with an ambience that has grown out of decades of wonderful work. A well-stocked library completes a room where one could lose oneself in the deposits of history and heritage. Layering is a key part of the development of evocative ideas for imagineers: seldom do they seek to produce just one single idea, rather lots of ideas that support a story.

STORYTELLING

Imagineers consider themselves as storytellers first and artists, architects or engineers second. Stories inform the design of the parks, and environments built on stories provide rich experiences for Guests (as visitors to the parks are known), drawing them deeper into the experience by appealing to all senses, inspiring their imagination, keeping them interested and ultimately generating multiple visits.

But the storytelling doesn't stop at the theme parks – imagineers build stories in their own workspaces too. 'You can tell a lot about a person from the way they set up their environment,' explains Dave Fisher, Senior Show Writer; 'people build their own stories in their rooms – it's an evolving process.' Imagineers have the freedom to surround themselves with things that serve to establish their own identity. Collected objects tell stories of exotic travels or act as trophies of recent work done. As with the parks, workplaces that are rich in stories will appeal to all senses, containing many layers that continually represent and stimulate the users in different ways, and thus allowing them to lose themselves in their own worlds. A storytelling environment is one that keeps people motivated about who they are and what they do day after day.

ABOVE The sculpture studio has a peaceful, almost 'spiritual' atmosphere – layers of history, craft and talent are lit by natural light that pours through huge windows.

RIGHT The team at Walt Disney Imagineering is made up from more than 140 different disciplines.

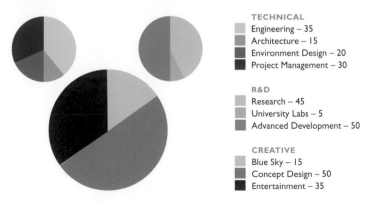

TECHNICAL
- Engineering – 35
- Architecture – 15
- Environment Design – 20
- Project Management – 30

R&D
- Research – 45
- University Labs – 5
- Advanced Development – 50

CREATIVE
- Blue Sky – 15
- Concept Design – 50
- Entertainment – 35

ABOVE AND OPPOSITE BELOW Ideas are brought to life through prototyping including life-sized test rigs for ride cars.

BELOW RIGHT Scale models are used as powerful communication tools for cross-disciplined teams.

OPPOSITE ABOVE The Creative Technology Lab is equipped with a virtual park walkthrough room that allows imagineers to experience and develop environments before they have been built.

BELOW The realism achieved in interactive Audio-Animatronics figures is made possible through a collision of traditional craft techniques and high technology – and lots of close collaboration.

CROSS-DISCIPLINES

Imagineers create new, realistic or fantasy worlds for the Disney theme parks by combining many different methods and techniques from many different perspectives. They embrace new technologies alongside traditional disciplines and techniques. With such a broad range of specialisations and skills, imagineers have found quick and effective ways of communicating their ideas through the collision of traditional scale models and computer-generated virtual reality.

Some of the most effective communication tools are the scale models you'll see decorating the studios and workshops. 'Some people think they're just pretty, but these models serve a really important purpose,' explains Hickman; 'they're a mainstay of our business – one of the best tools we have to convey information and ideas to many different disciplines.' You'll often see a team of imagineers huddling around a model of a new park or attraction, discussing the details of the ideas. 'Standing around the physical piece and communicating needs and thoughts is so powerful,' says Hickman. The ability for people from disparate backgrounds, approaching a problem from different perspectives, to speak a common language through physical models is extremely powerful, allowing back-and-forth integration and iteration of ideas that helps carry them from thoughts into reality.

At various stages in the process of creating a new environment, imagineers build and explore in the digital world: the Creative Technology Lab is equipped with a 7-foot-high curved screen, several virtual reality headsets, and a team of computer graphics specialists. Imagineers can walk virtually through the environments they're creating, testing out sightlines, perspective and scale to get a good idea of what a space will feel like to a Guest, before they begin to make them in the real world.

TOP High-speed, high-access areas allow quick
exchange of ideas, but are also furnished with
changing features to encourage moments to pause.

ABOVE The office of Senior Vice President of
Creative, Joe Rohde, whose travels to the Himalayas
have inspired many realistic details in theme parks.

SHARING IDEAS

At WDI there are many informal places and spaces to meet, collide and exchange ideas. Imagineering has what they proudly refer to as a 'hallway culture', and you'll often find an impromptu meeting or celebration taking place in the campus's corridors. The physical intersections near where people work are used for spontaneous gatherings. 'There's nothing better than a random, chance meeting,' remarks Jon Georges, Director of Creative Development. Creating these social, informal, agenda-less interactions is really important for forging connections between people – and for allowing ideas to float to the surface.

The 'Graffiti Hallway' was invented to maximise these chance meetings: a bare corridor between model shops that was originally an essential fire regulation has been turned into a place where imagineers and artists can display their work, paint on walls and pause for thought. The absence of furniture or clutter facilitates quick access between workshops, studios and offices, but the contents of the corridor (either painted straight onto the walls or mounted on wheels) are often changed and refreshed, prompting people to slow down and take in new information.

Of most importance to WDI teams is the opportunity to experiment, try things out, mock things up, and communicate ideas to each other as they're unfolding. And it's important to be able to do this quickly, ensuring that the energy behind the idea is not lost. An R&D 'rapid response team' of designers, engineers and project managers work together, sit together, eat together, all in the one building, with the ability to design, build and form anything that they need to – whether it be an interactive robot, or a social interaction wall that fosters creative collaboration synchronously across different locations and time zones! Environments last from just a week to a whole year, and can be reconfigured, broken down and changed at will. Extensive wireless systems on multiple levels support this fast-paced metamorphosis. Everything is intended to be fast, flexible and agile. The teams' mantra: 'Try it out, do it quick, see if it works, move on.'

There's a constant sense of creation at Imagineering – if something doesn't exist, someone will invent it. One of the tools that the R&D team has developed is a real-time, voice-recognition brainstorming room which 'listens in' to a conversation, pulling out key words and projecting search engine results and RSS feeds onto the wall to stimulate further ideas. 'Right now it's a little obnoxious,' says Scott Trowbridge, Vice President Creative, Research & Development, 'but we're working to make it a little more friendly.' Another new-to-the-world tool is an interactive collaboration tool that quickly connects imagineers, allowing them to know what others are working on at any given time.

The WDI spaces are far from plush and polished – they are well-equipped and full of activity. With literally thousands of ideas to every one that gets built, it is impossible

"YOU CAN'T TELL AN ARTIST WHEN TO GET
AN IDEA OR HOW MANY IDEAS TO GET."
John Hench

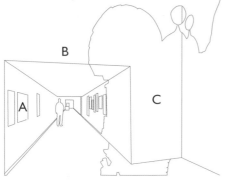

ABOVE 'Graffiti Hallway' is a great example of WDI's hallway culture, where many opportunities are created for informal collisions and meetings.

A. Art tributes painted directly onto the wall of the corridor.
B. Quotes from Walt and other 'Disney Legends' provide inspiration.
C. A lesson given by a guest artist in 'Forced Perspective' technique remains *in situ* for continued inspiration.

to get too attached to an idea – here people are encouraged to share, build and grow ideas to keep making them better and more appropriate. This easy-going, unpolished attitude towards the physical environment encourages a positive attitude towards failure, an important part of the creation process. There's a certain amount of risk associated with the expression of an idea – 'It's a personal statement,' remarks Jon Georges. 'We work tirelessly to create an environment where there really is no such thing as a bad idea; we allow all ideas to be expressed.'

Key to the approach is doing it all with a sense of fun. When people are having fun, they're more risk-tolerant. WDI does not just encourage play, but demands it. Play is a great vehicle for experimenting with failure: it's OK to mess up when you're playing a game – you just start over again, or reinvent the rules. 'We'll move the office around, go outdoors, start working backwards from the desired solution. We'll role-play. We'll do anything to find another way of thinking about things,' explains Trowbridge.

Walt Disney Imagineering's down-to-earth approach to thinking creatively about things that don't yet exist is supported by spaces that allow people from many different backgrounds to come together to share ideas in a relaxed, fun and playful way without fear of making a mess or getting it wrong.

OPPOSITE Playful imagineers do not think twice about taking a brainstorm session outdoors or onto a train (trainstorming), or changing the rules altogether.

BELOW An experiment with a prototype voice-recognition 'brainstorm room' that suggests stimulating information and imagery during ideation sessions.

FURTHER READING

The following is a shortlist of books, papers and websites that are informative for their approach to creativity and workplace design:

CREATIVITY AND INNOVATION IN BUSINESS

Tom Kelley & Jonathan Litmann, *The Art of Innovation: Lessons in Creativity from IDEO, America's Leading Design Firm*, Broadway Business, 2001

Tom Kelley, *The Ten Faces of Innovation: IDEO's Strategies for Beating the Devil's Advocate and Driving Creativity Throughout Your Organization*, Profile Business, 2008

AG Lafley & Ram Charan, *The Game-Changer: How You Can Drive Revenue and Profit Growth with Innovation*, Crown Business, first edition, 2008

Richard Branson, *Screw It, Let's Do It (Expanded Edition): 14 Lessons on Making It to the Top While Having Fun and Staying Green*, Virgin Books, revised and updated edition, 2008

Dave Allan, Matt Kingdon, Kris Murrin and Daz Rudkin, *Sticky Wisdom: How to Start a Creative Revolution at Work*, Capstone, second edition, 2002

Frans Johansson, *The Medici Effect: What Elephants and Epidemics Can Teach Us About Innovation*, Harvard Business School Press, first edition, 2006

Chris Baréz-Brown, *How to Have Kick Ass Ideas: Shake Up Your Business, Shake Up Your Life*, Skyhorse Publishing, 2008

Adrian Gostick and Scott Christopher, *The Levity Effect: Why It Pays to Lighten Up*, John Wiley & Sons, illustrated edition (28 March 2008)

Daniel H Pink, *A Whole New Mind: Why Right-Brainers Will Rule the Future*, Riverhead Trade, updated edition, 2006

Chip Heath & Dan Heath, *Made to Stick: Why Some Ideas Survive and Others Die*, Random House, first edition, 2007

GENERAL CREATIVITY

Mihaly Csikszentmihalyi, *Creativity: Flow and the Psychology of Discovery and Invention* (paperback), Harper Perennial, 1997

Michael J Gelb, *How to Think Like Leonardo Da Vinci: Seven Steps to Genius Every Day*, Dell, 2000

WORKPLACE DESIGN

IDEO, Colin Burns & Fred Dust, *Extra Spatial*, Chronicle Books, 2003

John Riordan & Kristen Becker, *The Good Office: Green Design on the Cutting Edge*, Collins Design, 2008

Franklin Becker and Fritz Steele, *Workplace by Design: Mapping the High-Performance Workscape*, Jossey-Bass, first edition, 1995

Marilyn Zelinsky, *The Inspired Workspace: Designs for Creativity and Productivity*, Rockport Publishers, illustrated edition, 2004

Turid H Horgen, Michael L Joroff, William L Porter & Donald A Schön, *Excellence By Design: Transforming Workplace and Work Practice*, John Wiley & Sons, first edition, 1998

Franklin Becker, *Offices at Work: Uncommon Workspace Strategies that Add Value and Improve Performance*, Jossey-Bass, first edition, 2004

Jeremy Myerson & Philip Ross, *Space to Work: New Office Design*, Laurence King Publishing, 2006

Teresa M Amabile, Regina Conti, Heather Coon, Jeffrey Lazenby & Michael Herron, 'Assessing the work environment for creativity', *The Academy of Management Journal*, Vol 39, No 5 (Oct 1996), pp 1154–84

Tore Kristensen, 'The physical context of creativity', *Creativity and Innovation Management*, Vol 13, No 2 (June 2004), pp 89–96

PICTURE CREDITS

The author and the publisher gratefully acknowledge the people who gave their permission to reproduce material in this book. While every effort has been made to contact copyright holders for their permission to reprint material, the publishers would be grateful to hear from any copyright holder who is not acknowledged here and will undertake to rectify any errors or omissions in future editions.